Survey for Assessing Racial/Ethnic Harassment and Discrimination in the U.S. Military

MIRIAM MATTHEWS, COREEN FARRIS, TERRY L. SCHELL,
KRISTIE L. GORE

RAND NATIONAL DEFENSE RESEARCH INSTITUTE

For more information on this publication, visit **www.rand.org/t/RRA1246-2**.

Published by the RAND Corporation, Santa Monica, Calif.

Library of Congress Cataloging-in-Publication Data is available for this publication.

ISBN: 978-1-9774-0789-4

Cover: Carlofranco/Istockphoto.

About This Research Report

The U.S. Department of Defense is committed to eliminating racial/ethnic harassment and discrimination among members of the U.S. armed forces. Assessment of racial/ethnic harassment and discrimination can clarify the nature and extent of these events and help support efforts to eliminate their occurrence. Further, Title 10, Section 481, of the U.S. Code mandates that the Department of Defense assess racial/ethnic harassment, racial/ethnic discrimination, and the climate of the military workplace. To meet these requirements, DoD fields the Workplace and Equal Opportunity Survey of Active Duty Members (WEOA) every four years and, on an alternating schedule, the Workplace and Equal Opportunity Survey of Reserve Component Members (WEOR) every four years. In preparation for the WEOR 2015, the Defense Manpower Data Center (DMDC)[1] and the former Office of Diversity Management and Equal Opportunity (ODMEO)[2] contracted the RAND Corporation to redesign a survey instrument included in the WEOA and WEOR.

To redesign this instrument, the RAND team reviewed survey research on racial/ethnic harassment and discrimination to identify promising items and measurement strategies. The team then worked with recognized experts in survey design and racial/ethnic harassment and discrimination to design the instrument. External experts, DMDC representatives, representatives from the former ODMEO, and representatives from the military services reviewed the instrument and provided feedback. This document contains information regarding the survey instrument, specific items and

---

[1] Responsibility for this and other surveys have since passed from DMDC to the Office of People Analytics.

[2] Following this contract and the development of the survey, ODMEO responsibilities were split between the Office of Diversity, Equity, and Inclusion and the Diversity Management Operations Center. ODMEO no longer exists as a DoD office.

scoring, and programming notes. The revised survey instrument has three modules that assess

- whether the respondent experienced racial/ethnic harassment
- whether the respondent experienced racial/ethnic discrimination
- for respondents who are categorized as experiencing racial/ethnic harassment or discrimination, the characteristics of the offenders, situations, and response systems.

The research reported here was completed in June 2021 and underwent security review with the sponsor and the Defense Office of Prepublication and Security Review before public release.

RAND National Security Research Division

This research was sponsored by DMDC and the former ODMEO and conducted within the Forces and Resources Policy Center of the RAND National Defense Research Institute, a federally funded research and development center sponsored by the Office of the Secretary of Defense, the Joint Staff, the Unified Combatant Commands, the Navy, the Marine Corps, the defense agencies, and the defense Intelligence Community.

For more information on the RAND Forces and Resources Policy Center, see www.rand.org/nsrd/ndri/centers/frp or contact the director (contact information is provided on the webpage).

Acknowledgments

We wish to thank staff members at the Defense Manpower Data Center who provided input on this project. We would also like to thank those in the Office of Diversity Management and Equal Opportunity, now Office for Diversity, Equity, and Inclusion, who supported, provided information to, and participated in discussions with us, including Norvel L. "Rock" Dillard, Beatrice Bernfeld, and Chad Schrecengost. In addition, We thank Lisa Jaycox, Jennifer Hawes-Dawson, Andrew Morral, Geoffrey McGovern, Kathy Sanders-Phillips, Veronica Venture, and Kim Hall for their comments on previous report drafts. We also thank Joseph G. Altonji of Yale University, William D. Crano of Claremont Graduate University, Eugene R. Fidell of Yale University, James M. Jones of the University of Delaware, and Felicia Pratto of the University of Connecticut for their contributions, thoughtful comments, and suggestions regarding the survey. We thank Eric Apaydin, Samantha Cherney, Dionne Barnes-Proby, Anita Szafran, and Barbara Hennessey of RAND for their assistance with survey item-bank development. We thank Lisa Jaycox, Jennifer Hawes-Dawson, Andrew Morral, Geoffrey McGovern, Kathy Sanders-Phillips, and Veronica Venture for their comments on previous report drafts.

Contents

Figures and Tables

Figures

Tables

Summary

The U.S. Department of Defense (DoD) is committed to eliminating harassment and unlawful discrimination within the U.S. armed forces. This includes harassment and discrimination on the basis of race or ethnicity, which persists across the United States, including in the U.S. military. To help military leaders and policymakers better understand the nature of racial/ethnic harassment and discrimination within the armed services, RAND researchers created a survey instrument to assess the prevalence of racial/ethnic harassment and discrimination within DoD. To do so, we (1) reviewed published surveys that assess racial/ethnic harassment, discrimination, microaggressions (i.e., stereotypes about specific races or ethnicities, passive poor treatment by others, and expressions of opinions regarding racism), and related content and (2) consulted with experts in the occurrence and measurement of harassment and discrimination on the basis of race/ethnicity.

This report provides a description of the development process used to design the survey instrument to assess racial/ethnic harassment and discrimination in the military and releases the full content and scoring procedures for the instrument. This information may help DoD policymakers better understand and interpret the survey results they receive. It can also assist analysts and survey research professionals with understanding the instrument design and with evaluating or conducting analyses of data collected using this instrument. In 2015, DoD adopted the instrument as part of the Workplace Equal Opportunity Surveys of military service members. The findings of their survey effort will continue to be released through official DoD channels. This report does not contain survey results.

Survey Design

The instrument includes three sections: assessments of the occurrence of racial/ethnic (1) harassment and (2) discrimination within the past year and, (3) for those who experience these offenses, assessment of the event, the offender, and the response system.

The Racial/Ethnic Harassment survey module begins with a brief set of instructions informing respondents that the questions will query "upsetting or offensive things that someone from work might have said or done that were related to your race/ethnicity" in the past year. Twelve screening items assess inappropriate workplace behaviors that were targeted at the respondent, at the respondent's racial/ethnic group, or at any other group. For any respondent who experienced one of the behaviors assessed in the screening items, follow-up questions determine whether the behavior was persistent (i.e., it continued even after the person who was doing it knew that it was upsetting to others) or was considered by the respondent to be severe (i.e., most people would know that the behavior would be offensive to service members in certain racial/ethnic groups). Anyone who indicates having experienced an inappropriate workplace behavior that was either persistent or severe is categorized as having experienced racial/ethnic harassment.

The Racial/Ethnic Discrimination survey module uses 12 screening items to assess whether a respondent has experienced a series of work-related harms, such as a poor performance review or assignment to undesirable tasks, as a result of his or her ethnicity or race. Any respondent who indicates experiencing a workplace harm in the past year and who indicates a source of information that would be admissible in court to support a claim of discrimination is categorized as having experienced racial/ethnic discrimination.

Figure S.1 summarizes the survey components used to determine whether the respondent experienced racial/ethnic harassment or discrimination in the past year. Although not all inappropriate behaviors identified in a survey are ultimately categorized as harassment or discrimination, DoD leadership will likely have an interest in trends in all inappropriate workplace behaviors, as well as trends in just those events that can be defined as racial/ethnic harassment or discrimination. The survey instrument can be scored to provide estimates for both.

FIGURE S.1
Flowchart of the Assessment of Racial/Ethnic Harassment and Discrimination

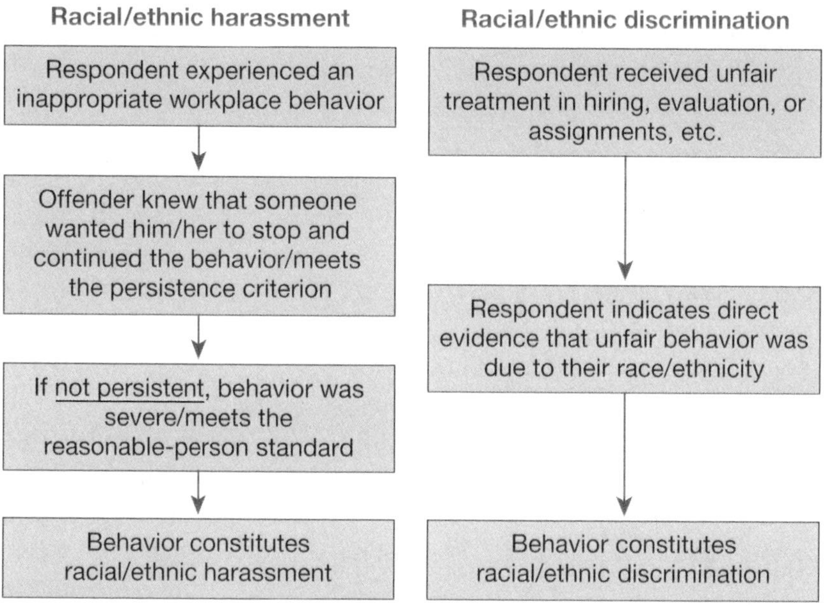

Recommendations

We recommend that reports of results from the survey administration provide estimates of the percentage of service members who, in the past year, experienced (1) racial/ethnic harassment, (2) racial/ethnic discrimination, (3) a Military Equal Opportunity (MEO) violation related to race and ethnicity (i.e., a combined category that includes all respondents who experienced either racial/ethnic harassment or discrimination), and (4) inappropriate workplace behaviors that do not meet the persistence or severity criteria. Although some inappropriate workplace behaviors experienced do not rise to the level of MEO violations, many military leaders will nonetheless note these behaviors as potential precursors to more-serious violations, evidence of poor discipline in the workplace, and potential barriers to inclusive work environments. Thus, to provide details on a range of potentially problematic behaviors in the military, reports based on this instrument should include the percentage of service members who experience inappropriate workplace behaviors and the percentage who have experiences that are categorized as racial/ethnic harassment, discrimination, or an MEO violation.

It will also be important to link the results of this survey instrument with either self-reported or administrative records of a respondent's race and ethnicity. The rate at which people of different racial and ethnic groups experience harassment and discrimination and their experiences with the response system after the violations occur almost certainly vary substantially, and a full understanding of harassment and discrimination within the military will require that these workplace violations be considered in the context of a respondent's race or ethnicity.

Section 481 of Title 10 of the U.S. Code requires that the Secretary of Defense conduct cross-service surveys to address racial/ethnic issues and discrimination among the U.S. armed forces. This law also requires that the Secretary of Defense report to Congress the results of this survey but does not require dissemination beyond Congress. However, widespread dissemination of results would allow this research to better assist policy development and change. We recommend that DoD clearly communicate the primary findings of the survey to a broader audience and describe the implications of these findings. Dissemination should be through channels that target audiences are most likely to use. Such channels could include web access to a full report of the results, web access to a summary report of the results, a press release, a newsletter, a newspaper article, an email alert, and a conference presentation. We recommend dissemination within 12 to 18 months after completion.

The services use periodic equal opportunity training to address multiple topics, including racial/ethnic harassment and discrimination (e.g., Defense Equal Opportunity Management Institute, 2013; Keller et al., 2015). Training programs across and within the services provide education about racial/ethnic harassment and discrimination, but the content varies. Many of the materials provided during these programs may not be based on research regarding the knowledge of and issues faced by service members. To better educate service members about racial/ethnic harassment and discrimination, information provided during equal opportunity training should draw on the results of this research effort. Prevalence estimates could provide a useful benchmark by which service members can understand their own and other service members' experiences.

The timeline of this survey-development effort precluded any cognitive pretesting or piloting of the survey instrument. We recommend that Office of People Analytics (OPA) staff review item and scale performance and update the survey as appropriate. For example, the list of barriers that may have prevented reporting harassment or discrimination currently has 21 items. It is possible that some of these items can be dropped for future fielding (e.g., if they are rarely endorsed or they duplicate another item). OPA and the Office of Diversity, Equity, and Inclusion will also be responding to a changing policy landscape as this survey is fielded in the future. As the needs of the end users morph, and as the realities of harassment and discrimination within the force change, the survey instrument should be revised.

Survey for Assessing Racial/Ethnic Harassment and Discrimination in the U.S. Military

Introduction

The U.S. Department of Defense (DoD) is committed to eliminating prohibited discrimination and harassment within the U.S. armed forces (Under Secretary of Defense for Personnel and Readiness, 2020b), and, as part of this effort, DoD seeks to measure the prevalence of these experiences among service members. Prohibited discrimination is defined as disparate treatment or harassment of an individual or group based on a prohibited factor contrary to federal law or regulation (Under Secretary of Defense for Personnel and Readiness, 2020c).[1] These discriminatory actions include, but are not limited to, denial of equal opportunities in recruitment, hiring, location assignment, training, promotion, and retention (Settles, Buchanan, and Yap, 2011).

Harassment is a form of discrimination (U.S. Equal Employment Opportunity Commission [EEOC], undated b), which DoD defines as "behavior that is unwelcome or offensive to a reasonable person, whether oral, written, or physical, that creates an intimidating, hostile, or offensive environment." To be racial/ethnic harassment, the unwelcome conduct would be based on race, color, or national origin (Under Secretary of Defense for Personnel and Readiness, 2020c).

The DoD definition of harassment for service members does not include specific examples of harassing behaviors. However, the DoD definition for

[1] These are actions that are not demonstrably related to business or organizational necessity. Protected categories in Title VII of the Civil Rights Act of 1964 (Pub. L. 88-352) are race, color, sex, religion, and national origin. Although these categories are not limited to racial/ethnic categories and, for some, there might be overlap among them (e.g., overlap between race and national origin), the present effort focuses on development of an assessment of racial/ethnic harassment and discrimination in the U.S. armed forces.

military employees who are civilians provides the following examples: unwanted physical contact, offensive jokes, epithets or name-calling, ridicule or mockery, insults or put-downs, displays of offensive objects or imagery, offensive nonverbal gestures, stereotyping, intimidating acts, and veiled threats of violence. Harassment becomes prohibited for service members in either of two circumstances: (1) when the conduct is persistent, such that continued employment involves continued exposure to the conduct; or (2) when the conduct is sufficiently severe or pervasive that a reasonable person would consider it hostile and offensive (Department of Defense Inspector General, 2019; EEOC, undated b).[2]

Racial/ethnic harassment and discrimination persist in the United States. In fiscal year 2020, the EEOC, the federal agency that enforces laws against unlawful U.S. workplace harassment and discrimination, received 67,448 discrimination charges from civilians (EEOC, undated a). Thirty-three percent of all charges filed were racial discrimination charges. The proportion of discrimination charges that were race based varied from 32.2 percent to 37.3 percent between 2004 and 2020 (EEOC, undated a). Not everyone who experiences racial/ethnic harassment and discrimination in the United States files charges (EEOC, 2005).

Workplace harassment and discrimination can have many negative consequences for both employees and organizations. Greater perceptions of experienced racial/ethnic harassment and discrimination are associated with lower job satisfaction, lower organizational commitment, greater intentions to leave, and fewer prosocial behaviors among employees (i.e., organizational citizenship behavior) (Ensher, Grant-Vallone, and Donaldson, 2001; Rhead et al., 2021; Sanchez and Brock, 1996; Shields and Price, 2002). Discriminatory and harassing workplace experiences are also associated with poorer physical and psychological health among employees (Triana, Jayasinghe, and Pieper, 2015). These results suggest that workplace

[2] Notably, in the companion cases of *Faragher v. City of Boca Raton*, 524 U.S. 775 (1998), and *Burlington Industries, Inc. v. Ellerth*, 524 U.S. 742 (1998), the U.S. Supreme Court established that an employer cannot be held liable for harassment if it can prove that it exercised reasonable care to prevent and address sexually harassing behavior or if the plaintiff employee failed to take advantage of available preventive or corrective opportunities that the employer provided.

racial/ethnic harassment and discrimination can be costly for organizations, such that these experiences can contribute to reductions in employee productivity, increases in employee absenteeism, and increases in organizational turnover (Triana, Jayasinghe, and Pieper, 2015).

DoD is aware of the multiple legal, individual, and organizational consequences of racial/ethnic harassment and discrimination and has communicated its commitment to promoting equal opportunity in the armed forces. As described in DoD Directive (DoDD) 1350.02, it is DoD policy to promote an environment that is free from prohibited discrimination because discrimination hinders combat readiness and mission accomplishment (Under Secretary of Defense for Personnel and Readiness, 2020b). DoDD 1350.02 also outlines the responsibilities of various entities, including the Military Equal Opportunity (MEO) program, the Defense Diversity Working Group, and the Defense Equal Opportunity Management Institute, to facilitate equal opportunity and eliminate discrimination and harassment in the armed forces. DoDD 1020.02E further outlines the implementation of diversity management and equal opportunity in DoD (Under Secretary of Defense for Personnel and Readiness, 2018). DoD's *Diversity and Inclusion Strategic Plan: 2012–2017* outlines goals for promoting diversity in DoD, including (1) ensuring leadership commitment to diversity; (2) employing a strategic outreach effort; and (3) developing, mentoring, and retaining talent (DoD, 2012b). Reiterating DoD's commitment to diversity, Secretary of Defense Lloyd Austin (Austin, 2021) recently stated,

> We maintain and enhance force readiness and develop the capabilities we need to protect America when we fully embrace a diversity of backgrounds, experiences, and thought. The Department will lead with our values, building diversity, equity, and inclusion into all aspects of our work and in everything we do. Inclusivity will drive innovative solutions across the enterprise and create a constructive environment in which every person has the space to contribute fully.

Quadrennial Survey Research

To quantify the extent of racial/ethnic harassment and discrimination in the military, DoD fields the quadrennial Workplace and Equal Opportunity Survey of Active Duty Members (WEOA) and Workplace and Equal

Opportunity Survey of Reserve Component Members (WEOR). These congressionally mandated surveys measure job satisfaction, professional climate (e.g., relationship with supervisors and coworkers), stress and well-being, racial/ethnic harassment, racial/ethnic discrimination, training, and beliefs about DoD's response to racial/ethnic harassment and discrimination. Respondents who report experiencing harassment or discrimination based on race or ethnicity are also asked about the circumstances, the role of the person responsible (e.g., peer, supervisor), and, if they reported the experience, the system's response.

The first survey was fielded in 1996 in response to the congressional mandate. In 2015, when RAND redesigned the survey metrics for racial/ethnic harassment and discrimination, the most recent publicly released reports were conducted with the Reserve Component in 2011 and active duty in 2013 (Defense Manpower Data Center [DMDC], 2014a; Namrow et al., 2014).[3] According to these reports, 8 percent of Reserve Component members had experienced racial/ethnic harassment or discrimination in their military jobs in the past year (DMDC, 2014a), and 10.2 percent of active-duty members indicated experiencing racial/ethnic harassment or discrimination in 2013 (Namrow et al., 2014). In 2013, active-duty minority members (15.9 percent) were more likely than white, non-Hispanic service members (6.5 percent) to indicate that they had experienced racial/ethnic harassment or discrimination in the past year (Namrow et al., 2014).

In the years before 2015, for a WEOA or WEOR to categorize a respondent as having experienced racial/ethnic harassment or discrimination, the respondent must have indicated having experienced negative workplace behavior and that they labeled their offensive or unfair experience or experiences as "racial/ethnic harassment" or "racial/ethnic discrimination" (Ormerod et al., 2007). This approach requires individual interpretation of the definitions, which leads to variability and imprecision in their measurement. Most people are not familiar with the details of equal employment opportunity law and MEO regulations, so many may miscategorize their experiences (Fitzgerald, Swan, and Fischer, 1995). For example, a service member exposed to pervasive, offensive racial comments and jokes from

[3] The active-duty report was not publicly available until after development of the survey measure described in this report.

colleagues might not label his or her experience as racial harassment even if it meets legal definitional criteria of a hostile workplace. Alternatively, a service member who is not recommended for promotion might perceive that lack of recommendation to be racial discrimination even if race did not play a role. Because this measurement approach makes the WEOA and WEOR measures sensitive to how knowledgeable the workforce is about regulations, there is a danger that effective training programs will appear to cause more harassment and discrimination over time as victims become better able to recognize and label their experiences correctly.

Similar measurement limitations were present in DoD's Workplace and Gender Relations (WGR) surveys, which DoD uses to assess sexual harassment and gender discrimination. In part to address these limitations, the WGR surveys underwent a significant revision in 2014 (Morral, Gore, and Schell, 2014), when DoD asked a RAND research team to redesign the WGR surveys to improve the validity of the survey results for sexual harassment. To do so, the RAND Military Workplace Study (RMWS) drew directly from criteria defining the MEO violations specified in DoDD 1350.2. Relative to past surveys that measured a construct better described as *psychological* or *perceived* sexual harassment (Fitzgerald, Swan, and Magley, 1997), the new approach offered greater precision in estimating the percentage of service members who experienced MEO violations as DoD defines them. Other survey changes included efforts to ensure that all reported events happened within the one-year time frame and to simplify question syntax in order to improve respondent comprehension.

One of the unintended consequences of the redesign of the WGR measure of sexual harassment and gender discrimination was that the WGR strategy to assess harassment and discrimination on the basis of gender fell out of alignment with the WEOA or WEOR strategy to measure harassment and discrimination on the basis of race or ethnicity. In the past, DMDC prioritized compatibility between the two measures (Ormerod et al., 2007). Thus, the former Office of Diversity Management and Equal Opportunity (ODMEO) and DMDC together requested that a RAND research team redevelop the WEOA and WEOR measures of racial/ethnic harassment and discrimination to bring them into alignment with existing DoD policies on these MEO violations and to create a degree of comparability with the WGR measures. The Office of People Analytics (OPA) began fielding the updated measures in the 2015 WEOR (Daniel, Namrow, et al., 2018) and requested that RAND release this measure development report at the same time the 2015 WEOR data were publicly released (to aid readers interested in how the new metrics were created). Unfortunately, public release was substantially delayed (Stewart, 2021), which in turn delayed this report.

This report describes the process by which RAND researchers redesigned the survey measures and publicly releases the survey items and scoring procedures (see Appendix A for the instrument and Appendix B for variable definitions). Given the time that has elapsed since we delivered the measures to DMDC and the former ODMEO, we have updated this report to reflect changes in policy since 2015 and to include research that has been published during this time period. Where conditions in 2015 affected measure development differently than would be the case in 2021, we make note of those influences. This report does not contain survey results, which are released through official DoD channels.

Study Approach

RAND researchers implemented a multipronged approach to design a survey instrument that DoD could use to estimate the percentage of service members who experienced racial/ethnic harassment and discrimination in the past year. This included a review of previous survey instruments designed to assess racial/ethnic harassment and discrimination, as well as items that DoD has used in the WEOA and WEOR. It also involved assembling a team of experts in survey design and in research on racial/ethnic harassment and discrimination. The RAND team discussed and submitted for review multiple instrument drafts to the expert team. Finally, the approach involved discussions with and review of survey elements by representatives from DMDC, the former ODMEO, and each of the services. We describe each of these elements in more depth in this section.

Review of Academic and Private-Sector Instruments

Previous survey instruments can provide information on commonly assessed dimensions and options provided to respondents. RAND researchers therefore reviewed previous surveys and developed a bank of items from these measures. To do so, we searched the following 15 databases:

- Academic Search Complete (EBSCO)
- Business Source Complete (EBSCO)
- Defense Technical Information Center
- Gannett Military Newsstand
- General Social Survey
- Inter-University Consortium for Political and Social Research
- iPOLL Databank (Roper Center)
- Military and Government Collection (EBSCO)
- Pew Research Center
- ProQuest Dissertations and Theses
- ProQuest Military Collection
- PsycARTICLES (American Psychological Association via EBSCO)
- PsycINFO (American Psychological Association via EBSCO)
- PsycNET/PsycTESTS (American Psychological Association)
- Social Sciences Abstracts (EBSCO).

We used the following search string:

> (race* OR racism OR racist OR racial OR ethnic* OR minorit*) AND (discriminat* OR harass* OR behavior* OR hassl* OR slur* OR insult* OR insensitiv*) AND (instrument* OR measur* OR scale* OR survey* OR questionnaire* OR empirical OR inventor*)

The asterisk is a wildcard used to address word variations (e.g., *measure, measures, measuring*).

Within these databases, we initially searched for sources published between 2000 and 2015. We limited the search to these years to ensure that we considered more-recent and more-relevant survey instruments. To reduce the possibility of missing older relevant instruments, we expanded the search by looking for scales mentioned in the works found through the formal search. Overall, we obtained 158 sources of information drawn from academic articles and dissertations, survey instruments (military, government, academic, and opinion polls), and white papers based on survey findings. We categorized survey questions based on whether they addressed harassment, discrimination, microaggressions, all three, or related content.[4] We categorized 535 items as addressing discrimination, 183 items on harassment, 633 on microaggressions, 71 as addressing all three of these, and 469 on other associated material.

During development of the survey instrument to assess racial/ethnic harassment and discrimination within DoD, we referenced the item bank as needed. Doing so allowed us to consider the wording and response options used in previous assessments of relevant constructs and ensure that the final instrument captured all necessary content.

In 2021, we repeated the aforementioned search and coding strategy, limited to the years 2015 to 2020 to capture relevant research that had been published since our original search. We identified 27 sources that included new scale items assessing racial/ethnic harassment or discrimination. We categorized 196 items as addressing discrimination, 31 items on harassment, 169 on microaggressions, and 14 on other associated material. On review, none of the newly identified scales offered a new approach that would necessitate redesigning the survey instrument delivered to DMDC and the former ODMEO in 2015.

Feedback from Academic Experts

Survey researchers often recommend that a team or panel of experts review and evaluate instrument drafts during survey design (Campanelli, 2008; Presser and Blair, 1994; Willis, Schechter, and Whitaker, 1999). Expert review can assist with identification of problematic survey language (e.g., instructions, question content or structure, response options or structure) (Rothgeb, Willis, and Forsyth, 2005). Further, research considering the value of expert review suggests that this method is one of the most productive available in terms of identification of survey questions that may reduce data quality (Olson, 2010; Presser and Blair, 1994; Rothgeb, Willis, and Forsyth, 2005).

[4] Microaggressions include stereotypes about specific races and ethnicities, passive poor treatment by others, and expressions of opinions regarding racism. Microaggressions tend to be subtle and, thus, might not rise to the standards of harassment and discrimination.

Accordingly, we assembled a panel of external experts with diverse research backgrounds to review drafts of the survey instrument. Two of our experts, James Jones and Felicia Pratto, have conducted and published extensive research on the psychology of prejudice and discrimination. Jones is a professor of psychology in the Department of Psychological and Brain Sciences and director of the Center for the Study of Diversity at the University of Delaware. He is the author of *Prejudice and Racism* (Jones, 1997) and cowrote the book *The Psychology of Diversity: Beyond Prejudice and Racism* (Jones, Dovidio, and Vietze, 2014). Pratto is a professor of social psychology at the University of Connecticut and coauthor of the book *Social Dominance: An Intergroup Theory of Social Hierarchy and Oppression* (Sidanius and Pratto, 1999).

William Crano also served on the panel as an expert with substantial experience in and knowledge of research on attitudes and research methodology. Crano is a professor of psychology at Claremont Graduate University and coauthor of multiple books, including *Principles and Methods of Social Research* (Crano, Brewer, and Lac, 2015). Joseph Altonji, a professor of economics at Yale University and author of multiple articles on wealth disparities, also provided feedback as a panel member. Finally, Eugene Fidell served on the panel as an expert in military law. He teaches at Yale Law School and has written extensively on U.S. military law.

The RAND team first developed a draft of the survey instrument to estimate the percentage of service members who experienced racial/ethnic harassment and discrimination. This draft built from the prior WEOA, WEOR, and other survey instruments (e.g., the WGR surveys). It identified items assessing racial/ethnic harassment and discrimination. After developing this draft, we submitted it to the expert panel for comments and then incorporated their feedback on items. For example, alterations were made to instruction wording, question wording, and question ordering. We then provided another draft for the experts to review, repeating this process as necessary.

Feedback from U.S. Department of Defense Experts

Following multiple rounds of revisions with our external experts, we asked military experts to review the draft survey instrument. In addition to reviewing the face and content validity of the instrument, the military reviewers appraised its tone, construction, and terminology for military suitability and cultural competence. We invited senior military representatives from each service branch and the Reserve Components with expertise in MEO policy and enforcement to review the survey. Representatives from DMDC and the former ODMEO also reviewed and submitted recommendations. We incorporated their suggestions as appropriate.

Study Limitations

Our effort had some limitations. This project had a short timeline that prevented use of several additional, frequently recommended survey design methods. Use of these methods may have further improved the survey instrument design. For example, we did not conduct cognitive pretesting, which involves asking respondents to verbalize their reactions to instrument instructions, questions, and response options and can help identify elements of an instrument that may contribute to respondent confusion or misunderstandings (Krosnick, 1999). We also did not undertake conventional pilot testing of the instrument. Pilot testing involves administering the survey to a sample of respondents that is similar to the one that will be asked to complete the final instrument under conditions similar to those in which the survey will be fielded. It can help to identify problems with the questionnaire structure, wording, length, skip patterns, and item coding (Krosnick and Presser, 2010). Similarly, we did not conduct comparability analyses to assess similarities and differences in results using different survey versions, nor did we conduct validity assessments of possible associations between instrument items and constructs that are associated with the criteria of interest (Alwin, 2010). In sum, given time constraints, we were unable to complete pretesting procedures that may have improved the measure.

Definitions for the constructs of interest within the U.S. armed forces were a challenge during initial survey design. Survey validity may be reduced when a measure is based on imprecisely defined constructs (Miller et al., 2009). In 2015, DoD did not have a standard definition of *racial/ethnic harassment*. To develop the measure of racial/ethnic harassment, we instead drew from the DoD definition of *sexual harassment* and the federal definition of *harassment* as a persistent or sufficiently severe activity to be reasonably considered hostile and offensive. Because the DoD definition of *unlawful racial/ethnic discrimination* also lacked detail regarding various behaviors and context, we obtained feedback from recognized experts and representatives in DoD. In 2020, updated DoD guidance expanded the policy definitions of *prohibited discrimination* and *harassment.* Fortunately, these more detailed descriptions aligned with the measure development decisions we made previously (as described in more detail later in the report) and no changes were required.

Finally, the survey items address experiences in the past year. As such, they do not account for people who experienced racial/ethnic harassment or discrimination in the military more than a year ago, who may continue to be affected by these experiences.

Survey Design

Clarification of Military Equal Opportunity Violations

The primary goal of the survey instrument is to assess the prevalence of racial/ethnic harassment and discrimination in the prior 12 months among service members. Designing such an instrument requires a working definition of the events that should be counted as racial/ethnic harassment or racial/ethnic discrimination. Ideally, these operational definitions would be closely aligned with the laws or regulations that define such incidents within this particular employment context.

However, the standard legal definitions of *workplace harassment* and *discrimination* used in civilian settings do not directly apply to the uniformed military services. The Civil Rights Act of 1964 forbids discrimination on the basis of specific, protected characteristics, including race, national origin, and sex. This act and its subsequent revisions provide the basis for the legal definition of *harassment* as a specific type of discrimination, a definition that has developed through federal regulations and case law. The Civil Rights Act states that it applies to "military departments"; however, the federal courts have interpreted this phrase as referring solely to the civilian employees of the military services (see, for example, *Gonzalez v. Department of the Army*, 718 F.2d 926 [9th Circuit, 1983]). Thus, although civilians who work for the military are covered by the standard legal definitions of *racial harassment* and *discrimination* derived from the Civil Rights Act, uniformed personnel, both active and reserve, are not.

Instead, at the time the measure was developed, uniformed service members were covered by military regulations that ban "unlawful discrimination" (DoDD 1350.2 [Under Secretary of Defense for Personnel and Readiness, 2015]). This regulation defined *unlawful discrimination* as "discrimination on the basis of color, national origin, race, religion, or sex that is not otherwise authorized by law or regulation." This very expansive, but vague, definition lacked the types of specific behavioral standards that exist in civilian law for identifying instances of discrimination or harassment. DoDD 1350.2 included a definition of *sexual harassment* (see ¶ E2.1.15). However, it did not contain comparable definitions for harassment based on race or the other protected characteristics. In addition, no legal precedents provided a more detailed interpretation of behavior that would constitute racial or ethnic discrimination or harassment under DoDD 1350.2 (likely because there are no provisions for money damages as a remedy under the regulation and so complaints are not handled through a judicial process).

Our efforts to develop a survey instrument to assess racial/ethnic harassment and discrimination were complicated by the lack of clear behavioral standards in the military regulations. Nearly any behavior that was not explicitly "authorized by law or regulation" could be considered discrimination under DoDD 1350.2. The RAND team, along with our external advisers, decided to assess a narrower definition of *racial/ethnic harassment* and *discrimination* than was described in DoDD 1350.2, ¶ E2.1.16. Specifically, we used a definition that was based on the standards for racial/ethnic harassment in a civilian context (under the Civil Rights Act of 1964 as revised) and closely parallels the definition of *sexual harassment* in DoDD 1350.2, ¶ E2.1.15.

This informed decision, guided by experts in the field, was subsequently validated by updated DoD guidance in 2020, which aligns with the details we initially inferred.

Our instrument separates racial/ethnic harassment from discrimination more broadly and assesses them in distinct survey modules (i.e., series of questions). Following the harassment and discrimination modules, a third and final module is designed only for those service members who experienced harassment or discrimination and assesses the characteristics of the situation, the offender, and the response system. A detailed description of each module follows.

Assessment of Racial/Ethnic Harassment

We sought to improve—where appropriate—the alignment between the WEOA and WEOR measures of racial/ethnic harassment and the recently updated WGR survey measures of sexual harassment (Morral, Gore, and Schell, 2014). The newly developed survey begins with a module addressing racial/ethnic harassment. In 2015, because there was no DoD policy definition of *racial/ethnic harassment*, we borrowed from the civilian standards for racial/ethnic harassment and the DoD definition of *sexual harassment* to create an operational definition of *racial/ethnic harassment* for this survey. We assumed that, for racial/ethnic harassment to be sufficient for DoD to take action, the experienced conduct would need to be only so pervasive or severe that a reasonable person would perceive the conduct to be hostile or offensive (Under Secretary of Defense for Personnel and Readiness, 2015) and it would not necessarily need to cause psychological harm. This inference was subsequently formalized in DoD Instruction 1020.03, which defined harassment as behavior that "is unwelcome or offensive to a reasonable person" and does not include a requirement that the behavior cause psychological harm (Under Secretary of Defense for Personnel and Readiness, 2020a).

The Racial/Ethnic Harassment module begins with a brief set of instructions that inform respondents that the next set of questions will query

> upsetting or offensive things that someone from work might have said or done that were related to your race/ethnicity. The questions ask about things that happened AFTER [date exactly one year before survey completion date].

The introductory instructions also provide a detailed definition of *someone from work*, which includes

> any person you have contact with *as part of your military duties.* "Someone from work" could be a supervisor, a civilian employee, contractor, or military personnel at any rank. They could be in your unit or in other units.

In addition, the instructions specify that incidents could have occurred on duty or off duty, on base or off base, provided that the person who instigated them was someone from work.

Given a long academic debate about the definitions of *race* and *ethnicity* (Omi and Winant, 2014) and the general consensus that these are socially defined, malleable, and shifting constructs (Nobles, 2000), we chose not to provide a definition of *race* or *ethnicity*. Instead, to clarify the constructs of interest, we provided example terms that respondents would likely find familiar. The instructions indicate that

> Race/Ethnicity refers to such terms for people as American Indian, Asian, Arab, Black, Filipino, Hispanic, Puerto Rican, Polish, White, and so on. A person can belong to one or more racial/ethnic groups.

We carefully selected example terms to include common terms and to prompt respondents to consider ethnic groups that they might not otherwise be primed to consider (e.g., Arab, Polish). All examples are protected classes according to Title VII of the Civil Rights Act of 1964. Following the instruction page, the Racial/Ethnic Harassment module begins with 12 screening questions assessing inappropriate workplace behaviors that, if experienced, could indicate that racial/ethnic harassment had occurred (Table 1.1, items H1–H12). Any respondent who reports not experiencing any of these 12 inappropriate workplace behaviors in the past year receives no further questions in this module.

Any respondent who indicates in screening items H1 to H10 and H12a having experienced inappropriate workplace behavior receives follow-up questions to determine whether the behavior was either (1) persistent (i.e., it continued even after the person who was doing it knew that it was upsetting to others) or (2) considered by the respondent to be severe (i.e., a reasonable person would know that the behavior would be offensive to service members in certain racial/ethnic groups).

Figure 1.1 illustrates the flow of follow-up questions and the logic for final categorization of conduct constituting an MEO violation.

Each respondent receives up to three follow-up questions to assess whether the behavior experienced was persistent or severe. For ease of responding, persistence is measured with two questions. The first assesses whether the respondent believes that the offender was aware that the behav-

TABLE 1.1
Racial/Ethnic Harassment Screening Items

Item Identifier	Item	Target of Behavior
H1	Since [X date], has someone from work made you uncomfortable, angry, or upset by telling racial/ethnic jokes?	Any group
H2	Since [X date], has someone from work used a racial/ethnic term that made you uncomfortable, angry, or upset? For example, an offensive label such as *spic*, *nigger*, *raghead*, *Polack*, or *cracker*.	Any group
H3	Since [X date], has someone from work made you uncomfortable, angry, or upset by claiming that their race/ethnicity is better than others?	Any group
H4	Since [X date], has someone from work made you uncomfortable, angry, or upset by displaying something that threatens or insults a racial/ethnic group? This includes tattoos, emails, pictures, flags, or anything that insults racial/ethnic groups or refers to racial supremacy groups.	Any group
H5	Since [X date], has someone from work made you uncomfortable, angry, or upset by insulting your racial/ethnic group?	Respondent's racial/ethnic group
H6	Since [X date], has someone from work made you uncomfortable, angry, or upset by using a stereotype about your racial/ethnic group? Stereotypes are beliefs about the characteristics of group members—for example, that they tend to be cheap, aggressive, or shy.	Respondent's racial/ethnic group
H7	Since [X date], has someone from work made you uncomfortable, angry, or upset by making a comment about a physical characteristic of your racial/ethnic group? This might be, for example, a comment about your skin color, height, hair, or eye shape.	Respondent's racial/ethnic group
H8	Since [X date], has someone from work made you uncomfortable, angry, or upset by making a comment about the way people in your racial/ethnic group talk?	Respondent's racial/ethnic group
H9	Since [X date], has someone from work made you uncomfortable, angry, or upset by showing you a lack of respect because of your race/ethnicity?	Respondent
H10	Since [X date], has someone from work made you uncomfortable, angry, or upset by excluding you from an activity because of your race/ethnicity?	Respondent
H11	Since [X date], has someone from work threatened or physically assaulted you because of your race/ethnicity?	Respondent
H12	We have asked you questions about how someone from work might have created difficulties for you. We are also interested in whether someone from work targeted another person based on their race/ethnicity. Since [X date], has someone from work directed an offensive action or comment at another person because of their race/ethnicity?	Another person
If yes to H12, H12a	Did that action or comment make you uncomfortable, angry, or upset?	Another person

FIGURE 1.1
Flowchart of the Assessment of Racial/Ethnic Harassment and Discrimination

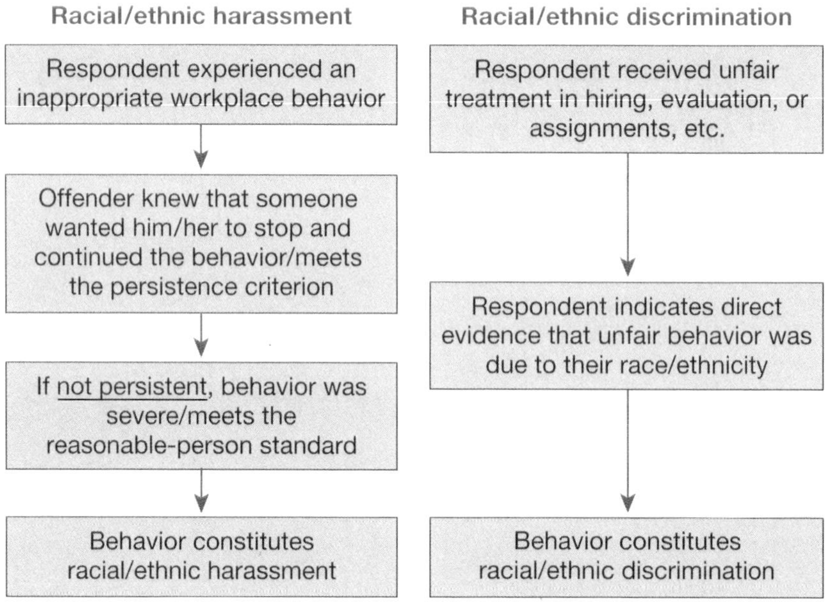

ior was unwelcome. The item text is, "Do you think they ever knew that you or someone else wanted them to stop? If more than one person did this, do you think any of them ever knew?" If the respondent reports believing that the offender was aware that someone was offended by the behavior, the second question asks, "Did they continue [the inappropriate behavior] even after they knew that you or someone else wanted them to stop?"[5] If the respondent indicates that the behavior persisted even after the offender was aware that someone wanted them to stop, the experience meets the persistence criterion, and the respondent is classified as having experienced racial/ethnic harassment.

Inappropriate workplace behavior that was not persistent might still constitute racial/ethnic harassment if a reasonable person would consider it severe. Severity was assessed via the item "Do you think most people know

[5] The phrase in brackets was specific to the screening question assessed.

that this behavior would be offensive to service members in certain racial/ethnic groups?" A service member who responds yes to this follow-up item is classified as having experienced racial/ethnic harassment.

Any respondent who indicates in screening item H11 that "someone from work threatened or physically assaulted you because of your race or ethnicity" does not receive follow-up questions. Such an incident would constitute a hate crime and is, by definition, severe. It meets the reasonable-person standard in that it is classified as a criminal offense under the Uniform Code of Military Justice (DoD, 2012a). Therefore, it does not need additional follow-up items to determine whether it rises to the level of an MEO violation.

Scoring

Any respondent endorsing any of the 12 racial/ethnic harassment screening questions is categorized as having experienced inappropriate workplace behavior. Such experiences are further categorized as racial/ethnic harassment, specifically, if the offensive behavior either (a) persisted after the person exhibiting the behavior knew that the respondent or other people wanted it to stop or (b) was sufficiently severe that, in the respondent's opinion, most people would know that it would be offensive to service members in certain racial/ethnic groups. These two criteria are designed to rule out instances in which respondents themselves realize that the offender had no way of knowing that the behavior could create a hostile work environment. Note that one behavior (measured in item H11) might also rise to the level of a hate crime, but this instrument does not assess whether the experience would meet the legal definition of *hate crime*. Instead, it specifies that the experience constitutes, at a minimum, racial/ethnic harassment.

Racial/ethnic harassment can occur when the harassing behavior is targeted at (1) the respondent, (2) the respondent's racial/ethnic group, or (3) people of a different racial/ethnic group from the respondent's. Provided that the respondent indicates being "uncomfortable, angry, or upset" by the behavior and the behavior was either persistent or severe, it constitutes harassment.

To better understand each respondent's experiences, it may be helpful to create derived variables that separate harassment experiences into these three types of targets. Respondents who are categorized as experiencing racial/ethnic harassment on the basis of item H9, H10, or H11 constitute service members who experienced racial/ethnic harassment that was targeted directly at the respondent. Respondents who are categorized as experiencing racial/ethnic harassment on the basis of item H5, H6, H7, or H8 constitute service members who experienced racial/ethnic harassment that was targeted at the respondent's racial/ethnic group. For items H1 to H4 and H12, it is not immediately clear whether the harassment that the respondent experienced was directed at his or her own racial/ethnic group or people of another racial/ethnic group. Thus, any respondent who is categorized as experiencing harassment on the basis of one or more of these items receives a follow-up question that assesses whether the harassment was directed at the person's racial/ethnic group, someone else's racial/ethnic group, or both. Answers to this item should be used to correctly subcategorize the target of the harassment and, therefore, finalize the derived variable that describes the target of the harassment for each respondent who experienced harassment.

Finally, to understand how respondents perceive the events they experienced, a follow-up question assesses whether the respondent considered those experiences to be racial/ethnic harassment (item RH_F1; see Appendix A). This item should not be used to categorize a respondent as having experienced racial/ethnic harassment. Some service members are not fully knowledgeable about the legal standards associated with harassment and may minimize their experiences, believing that they were not "serious enough" to rise to the level of an MEO violation or, alternatively, perceive minor workplace infractions that are not persistent or severe enough to be MEO violations. Although this item will provide useful data to assess whether service members have been adequately trained to correctly categorize their own experiences, the previous screening and follow-up items are sufficient to categorize experiences as racial/ethnic harassment.

Assessment of Racial/Ethnic Discrimination

The survey module on racial/ethnic discrimination uses 12 screening items to assess whether a respondent has experienced a series of work-related harms as a result of his or her race or ethnicity. For any respondent reporting a work-related harm, a follow-up item assesses whether the evidence to support the claim that the workplace harm was due to race or ethnicity would be admissible in court. Any respondent who indicates having experienced a workplace harm in the past year and who indicates a source of information that would be admissible to support a claim of discrimination is categorized as having experienced racial/ethnic discrimination in the past year.

The Racial/Ethnic Discrimination module follows the harassment module and begins with brief instructions that direct respondents to consider their experiences with workplace discrimination:

> The next questions ask if someone from work treated you unfairly because of your race/ethnicity, and if they would have treated someone of a different race/ethnicity better.

The screening items assess several military work domains in which a respondent may have experienced racial/ethnic discrimination (Table 1.2). Any respondent who denies experiencing any form of work-related discrimination in the past year receives no further questions in this module.

Any respondent who indicates having experienced a work-related harm in the past year receives a series of follow-up items that assesses the type of evidence the respondent used to infer that the harm was due to the respondent's race or ethnicity (Table 1.3). A respondent is categorized as having experienced racial/ethnic discrimination if the respondent indicates that the offending person made a comment that shows that race or ethnicity was taken into account (RDXb), did or said something that showed that they dislike the

TABLE 1.2

Racial/Ethnic Discrimination Follow-Up Items

Item Identifier	What Led You to Believe That the Person [Caused the Work-Related Harm] Because of Your Race/Ethnicity? Select All That Apply
RDXb	The person made a comment showing they took your race/ethnicity into account. (Yes or No)
RDXc	The person said or did something showing that they dislike your racial/ethnic group. (Yes or No)
RDXd	The person treated you worse than other people in the same situation who were of a different race/ethnicity. (Yes or No)
RDXe	You suspect it was due to your race/ethnicity because it is common for people in the military to mistreat people of your race/ethnicity. (Yes or No)

TABLE 1.3
Racial/Ethnic Discrimination Screening Items

Item Identifier	Item
RD1	Since [X date], did someone give you a lower military performance evaluation because of your race/ethnicity?
RD2	Since [X date], did someone make it harder for you to get a military award because of your race/ethnicity? This includes ribbons, medals, coins, quarterly or annual awards, decorations, and commendations.
RD3	Since [X date], did someone make it harder for you to get a military promotion because of your race/ethnicity?
RD4	Since [X date], did someone from the military make it difficult or impossible for you to go into your preferred military occupation because of your race/ethnicity? For example, your preferred MOS, career field, [Air Force specialty code], or rating.
RD5	Since [X date], did someone assign you to an undesirable military unit, installation or country because of your race/ethnicity?
RD6	Since [X date], did someone assign you to either undesirable or unimportant military tasks because of your race/ethnicity?
RD7	Since [X date], did someone make it difficult or impossible to get a military training opportunity because of your race/ethnicity?
RD8	Since [X date], did someone give you an unfair score on a military training evaluation because of your race/ethnicity?
RD9	Since [X date], did someone deny your military leave or pass/liberty request because of your race/ethnicity?
RD10	Since [X date], did someone from the military punish you unfairly because of your race/ethnicity?
RD11	The military provides many types of services and benefits to service members, such as medical care, military housing, recreation centers, commissaries, and so on. Since [X date], did someone at one of these places provide worse service or fewer benefits because of your race/ethnicity?
RD12	Since [X date], did someone from the military restrict your options for scheduling your drill days or military training because of your race/ethnicity?

NOTE: MOS = military occupational specialty.

respondent's racial/ethnic group (RDXc), or treated the respondent worse than others in the same situation who were of a different racial/ethnic group (RDXd). Any respondent who does not have any of these types of admissible evidence but indicates suspecting that the workplace harm was due to the respondent's race or ethnicity (item RDXe) is not categorized as having experienced discrimination. However, the respondent is still described as having experienced inappropriate workplace behavior.

Scoring

Any respondent endorsing any of the 12 racial/ethnic discrimination screening questions is categorized as having experienced inappropriate workplace behavior. The experience is further subcategorized as racial/ethnic discrimination, specifically, if the respondent cites admissible evidence that the behavior causing the work-related harm was due to their race or ethnicity (item RDXb, RDXc, and RDXd). Although respondents who do not cite clear evidence that the work-related harm was based on their race or ethnicity are not categorized as experiencing discrimination, it should not be concluded that their experience was definitively not discrimination, only that the evidence available via a survey was not sufficient to make the inference. This type of suspected workplace harm that is not explicitly linked to race or ethnicity by the offender (e.g., lower promotion rates for equally qualified black service members) can be better uncovered and established via statistical techniques examining an entire workforce.

To understand how respondents perceive the events they experienced, a follow-up question assesses whether the respondent considered his or her experiences to be racial/ethnic discrimination (item RD_F1). This item should not be used in scoring procedures. Some service members are not fully knowledgeable about the legal standards associated with discrimination and may minimize their experiences, believing that they were not "serious enough" to rise to the level of MEO violations or, alternatively, perceive minor workplace infractions that are not persistent or severe to be MEO violations. Although this item will provide useful data to assess whether service members have been adequately trained to correctly categorize their own experiences, the screening and follow-up items alone are sufficient to categorize an experience as racial/ethnic discrimination.

Assessment and Scoring of Racial/Ethnic Military Equal Opportunity Violations

Racial/ethnic MEO violation is an umbrella term that can include both racial/ethnic harassment and racial/discrimination. Any respondent who is scored as having experienced racial/ethnic harassment, racial/ethnic discrimination, or both should be included as having experienced a racial/ethnic MEO violation.

Assessment of the Situation, Offender Characteristics, and Response System

For respondents who are categorized as experiencing racial/ethnic harassment, racial/ethnic discrimination, or both, a series of follow-up questions assesses the characteristics of the situation and the offender (e.g., gender, race or ethnicity, military rank). If a respondent indicates having reported the situation to someone in the military who is obligated to address the harassment or discrimination, additional items assess the respondent's experiences with the military response system. If the respondent chose not to report the situation to a military authority, a series of questions assesses barriers to reporting. We modeled follow-up items on items developed for the RMWS (Morral, Gore, and Schell, 2014) and included on subsequent WGR surveys.

The WEOA and WEOR also included a series of follow-up questions for service members who experienced harassment or discrimination. Of the 70 follow-up items included in the most recent publicly released fielding of the WEOR (DMDC, 2014b), our revised version retained 4 items exactly as written (6 percent).

We retained 23 of the 70 items with minor alterations to item wording that did not change the basic content of the question (33 percent). Most of these changes were either simple grammatical changes that clarified the question or improved question fit within the revised survey structure. For example, a question assessing barriers to reporting was changed from "You did not know how to report" to "You did not know how to report it." Other changes in this group included small points of clarification; for example, a question assessing when the events took place was changed from "While you were deployed?" to "Did it ever occur while you were deployed to a combat zone or to an area where you drew imminent danger pay or hostile fire pay?"

We retained 14 of the 70 WEOA and WEOR follow-up items but revised them significantly such that the content, although similar, has changed (20 percent). For example, a WEOA and WEOR question asked whether the respondent "[told] the person(s) to stop." Because respondents could ask for a variety of resolutions from an offender (in addition to simply stopping), we changed this item to read, "Did you discuss this situation with the person(s) who did the upsetting or unfair things?"

Finally, we dropped 29 of the 70 WEOA and WEOR follow-up items from the survey (41 percent). Most of these items were not retained because they applied to a small number of respondents and, as a result, the survey would lack the precision to reliably estimate the proportion of respondents who experienced the event. For example, understanding retaliation experienced by service members who report racial harassment or discrimination is very important. However, this survey effort will have too few respondents to reliably estimate the percentage of service members who experienced harassment or discrimination, chose to report it, and subsequently experienced retaliation for reporting.

The final set of questions assessing the situation, offender, and response system included the 41 items that were the same as or similar to questions previously fielded in the WEOA surveys and 53 items that we added (94 questions total). Not all questions apply to all respondents; for example, items assessing barriers to reporting are presented only to those respondents who chose not to report their experiences to someone tasked with enforcing MEO policies. Many of the additional items are items that parallel follow-up items included in the biennial WGR surveys of active and reserve personnel on sexual harassment and gender discrimination. Additional items include questions to learn the rank of the offender or offenders, assess workplace consequences of the harassment or discrimination (e.g., "Did this situation ever make your workplace less productive or compromise your unit's mission?"), assess psychological health symptoms that the experiences may have triggered (e.g., "Did this situation make you have trouble sleeping or give you nightmares?"), and determine additional system responses to a report (e.g., "Someone talked to the [person or people] to ask them to change their behavior").

Department of Defense Implementation of Survey Measures

RAND delivered the survey items and programming instructions to DMDC and the former ODMEO in 2015. DMDC, and later OPA, subsequently included the racial/ethnic harassment and racial/ethnic discrimination screening items in their fielding of the 2015 WEOR and the 2017 WEOA (Daniel, Namrow, et al., 2018; Daniel, Claros, et al., 2019). In the report on the 2015 survey, they state,

> As agreed, the RAND Corporation was contracted by DMDC and the former ODMEO to construct a new measure of racial/ethnic harassment and/or racial/ethnic discrimination by modifying the current congressionally approved measure of gender discrimination and harassment used in the *2014 RAND Military Workplace Survey* and *2015 Workplace and Gender Relations Survey of Reserve Component Members* conducted by OPA to apply to experiences based on race/ethnicity. Beginning with *2015 WEOR*, the prior measure of racial/ethnic harassment and racial/ethnic discrimination was replaced with this new metric. (Daniel, Namrow, et al., 2018, p. v–vi)

Public release of the report was delayed until 2021 (Stewart, 2021). DoD researchers chose to categorize service members as experiencing "racial/ethnic harassment" if they experienced one or more of the screening items describing inappropriate workplace behaviors (Daniel, Namrow, et al., 2018). Our recommendation had been to conclude that an experience constituted "racial/ethnic harassment" only if the respondent indicated that the behavior was severe (meeting a reasonable-person standard) or persistent (continued after the person knew that it was unwelcome). Similarly, in the DoD report, service members were categorized as experiencing "racial/ethnic discrimination" if they experienced one or more of the screening items describing inappropriate workplace behaviors (Daniel, Namrow, et al., 2018). This contrasts with our recommendation that discrimination be coded only when the respondent indicated an admissible form of evidence (e.g., a comment that shows race/ethnicity was taken into account) rather than a suspicion that the workplace harm was due to race or ethnicity. Based on conversations with stakeholders, we understand that DoD attorneys recommended against using the persistence, reasonable-person, or admissible-evidence standards for categorization, because these criteria were developed in civilian settings. They recommended that these additional thresholds not be applied to the DoD estimates of racial/ethnic harassment and discrimination, essentially selecting a lower threshold for identifying behavior as harassing or discriminatory. We recommend that this decision be revisited in light of newer DoD policy guidance.

Using this modified threshold, DoD reported that 3.9 percent of Reserve Component members had experienced racial/ethnic discrimination in the past year, and 12.8 percent had experienced racial/ethnic harassment in the past year (Daniel, Namrow, et al., 2018). A total of 14.8 percent experienced either racial/ethnic discrimination or racial/ethnic harassment. Black service members (26.1 percent) were more likely than members of other racial/ethnic groups to experience racial/ethnic harassment or discrimination. These percentages correspond only to experiences in the military workplace, which, for most Reserve Component members, is not a full-time duty.

For active-duty service members, DoD reported that 5.6 percent of service members had experienced racial/ethnic discrimination, and 16.5 percent had experienced racial/ethnic harassment in the past year (Daniel, Claros, et al., 2019). A total of 17.9 percent experienced either racial/ethnic discrimination or racial/ethnic harassment. Black (31.2 percent) and Asian (23.3 percent) service members were more likely than members of other racial/ethnic groups to experience racial/ethnic harassment or discrimination.

Neither the 2015 WEOR nor the 2017 WEOA included the RAND updated follow-up items that assess the characteristics of the situation, offender, and response experiences. Follow-up items were retained as written in the WEOR and WEOA before 2015.

Recommendations

Lessons learned during the design process for this survey and through our review of similar instruments suggest several actions that DoD; the Office of Diversity, Equity, and Inclusion; and OPA, specifically, could take as part of their survey research efforts addressing racial/ethnic harassment and discrimination.

Report the Results in a Way That Will Be Most Informative to Congress, the Department of Defense, and Each Service

We recommend that reports using this survey instrument provide estimates of the percentages of service members who, in the past year, experienced (1) racial/ethnic harassment, (2) racial/ethnic discrimination, (3) an MEO violation related to race or ethnicity (i.e., harassment or discrimination), and (4) inappropriate workplace behaviors. As the survey is currently administered, prevalence of inappropriate workplace behaviors is being described as "racial/ethnic harassment," for example, even if those inappropriate behaviors are not persistent or severe. In light of recent policy revisions, DoD should consider revisiting this decision and either (a) return the requirement that the behavior meet the persistence or severity criterion in order for a respondent to be categorized as experiencing "racial/ethnic harassment," or (b) describe the results as a measure of "inappropriate workplace behavior."

It will also be important to continue to link the results of this survey instrument with either self-reported or administrative records of the respondent's race or ethnicity. The rate at which people of different race or ethnicity groups experience harassment and discrimination and their experiences with the response system after the violations occur almost certainly vary substantially, and a full understanding of harassment and discrimination within the military will require that these workplace violations be considered in the context of a respondent's race or ethnicity. We recommend that DoD continue its current practice of reporting survey results separately, at a minimum, by the Office of Management and Budget race and ethnicity categories (Office of Management and Budget, 2006).

Widely Disseminate the Results of Each Survey Wave in a Timely Manner

A fundamental aspect in the utilization of research results is information dissemination (e.g., Bowen and Zwi, 2005; Gagnon, 2011; Wilson et al., 2010). Section 481 of Title 10 of the U.S. Code requires that the Secretary of Defense conduct cross-service surveys to address racial/ethnic issues and discrimination in the U.S. armed forces. This law also requires that the Secretary of Defense report to Congress the results of this survey but does not require dissemination beyond Congress. Timely and widespread dissemination of results beyond Congress, however, will allow this research to better assist policy development and change. Researchers should provide clear and concise information about their survey results to those who choose to participate in their work (Fernandez, Kodish, and Weijer, 2003). Distributing the results of each survey wave to members of the armed forces (i.e., the population sampled) demonstrates respect for participants' time and input, improves transparency about these issues, and allows military leaders to be better informed when making or implementing policy changes (MacNeil and Fernandez, 2007). Distributing survey results beyond the armed forces can also assist various decisionmakers to develop new policy ideas and improve practices (Lomas, 1997).

When disseminating survey results, DoD should clearly communicate the primary findings and the implications of these findings to the target audiences, as described in a separate recommendation. Dissemination should be through channels that target audiences are most likely to use. Such channels might include a full report of the results accessible via the web, a summary report of the results accessible via the web, a press release, a newsletter, a newspaper article, an email alert, and a conference presentation (Wilson et al., 2010), and dissemination should occur in a timely manner (Lomas, 1997). We recommend dissemination within 12 to 18 months after completion.

Use the Results to Develop and Improve Efforts to Prevent Harassment and Discrimination in the U.S. Armed Forces

The services use periodic equal opportunity training to address multiple topics, including racial/ethnic harassment and discrimination (e.g., Defense Equal Opportunity Management Institute, 2013; Keller et al., 2015).

Training programs across and within the services provide variable information regarding racial/ethnic harassment and discrimination. Many of the materials provided during these programs might not be based on research regarding the knowledge of issues that service members face. To better educate service members about racial/ethnic harassment and discrimination, the information provided during equal-opportunity-relevant training should draw from the results of this research effort. Basic prevalence estimates could provide a useful benchmark by which service members can understand their own and other service members' experiences.

The survey results could serve as a form of needs assessment that addresses service members' experiences and perceptions. By drawing on the results, equal opportunity and similar training can be tailored to address the conduct and perceptions most relevant to service members. Most training programs aimed at addressing diversity issues do not adapt training to a particular organizational context or people within this context. Training that is tailored to the participants is more likely to be effective than training that does not consider participant perceptions or experiences (Roberson, Kulik, and Pepper, 2003).

Data regarding the harassing and discriminatory conduct that service members experience can be used to tailor training to address more–frequently experienced behaviors. For example, training could focus on more-common forms of racial/ethnic harassment or discrimination and provide explicit messages that the armed forces do not tolerate these behaviors. Results about the characteristics of the person or group who performed the behavior can also guide training. If those at certain ranks are more likely than others to harass or discriminate against others, those in these ranks might need more-frequent and more-thorough training. Information regarding reporting and perceptions of the actions that were taken after reporting may also be useful in training provided to leaders. Specifically, this information could help increase leader awareness of reporting barriers and appropriate responses to reports of racial/ethnic harassment and discrimination. Finally, groups that are particularly likely to misclassify their harassment experiences as not constituting harassment may require targeted training to help them better understand the parameters that define racial/ethnic harassment within the military.

Revise the Survey and Survey Methods as Necessary

OPA, the DoD agency that currently manages and reports results from the WEOA and WEOR, has a strong record of best practices in survey sample design (e.g., DMDC, 2012a; DMDC, 2012b). We are confident that the OPA team will design a sampling strategy that will ensure that adequate numbers of service members in each racial/ethnic group respond to the survey (and adequate numbers from service branches and pay grades in each group). This will ensure that estimates of racial/ethnic harassment and discrimination within each reportable category are sufficiently precise to guide decisionmaking and track trends over time.

From our experience implementing the RMWS, we have found that survey fatigue and drop-off can be a problem in surveys such as this. Respondents who may have been willing to complete the survey grow weary after 10 or 15 minutes of responding to questions and discontinue the survey. For this reason, it is preferable that the most critical or most informative measures be placed early in the survey, and less critical measures be placed later. We recommend that the measures of racial/ethnic harassment and discrimination be located as near to the beginning of the WEOR and WEOA as possible.

The timeline of this survey development effort precluded any cognitive pretesting or piloting of the survey instrument. After the first use of survey items, we recommend that DMDC/OPA staff review item and scale performance and update the survey as appropriate. For example, the list of barriers that may have prevented reporting harassment or discrimination is currently 21 items long. It is possible that some of these items can be dropped for future fielding (e.g., if they are rarely endorsed or they duplicate another item). OPA and the Office of Diversity, Equity, and Inclusion will also be responding to a changing policy landscape as this survey is fielded in the future. As the needs of the end users change, and as the realities of harassment and discrimination within the force change, the survey instrument should be revised.

Conclusion

Assessing the extent of racial/ethnic harassment and discrimination in the military, as well as related inappropriate workplace behaviors, poses many challenges. People experiencing such behaviors may not know whether the behavior is legally appropriate or permitted by regulations or what may not be strictly of legal concern but still inappropriate. This survey instrument provides a means to better assess these MEO violations. The RAND research team developed a survey instrument that can provide estimates of racial/ethnic discrimination, racial/ethnic harassment, and related inappropriate workplace behaviors that have occurred in the past year. The survey will provide military leaders and policymakers with an assessment of current problems and trends in those events over time. Limitations of the instrument include the lack of pilot testing. Military researchers and survey experts at OPA can, however, adjust the questionnaire after the initial fielding. The item bank developed for this work provides alternative versions of questions, as well as questions assessing topics not included in the final RAND survey instrument.

APPENDIX A

Survey Instrument

This appendix provides the content of the survey instrument.

Programming Notes

- Programming notes are in blue.
- Variables and response values are in red.
- To enhance readability, limit the screen width of question text. Do not use scrolling pages.
- Unless specified otherwise, every respondent receives each question. If the stems are the same, place one question per page or more.
- Item formatting appears as suggested for the final survey. All questions appear in **bold**, with added explanatory sentences not bolded (i.e., roman type), and words or phrases emphasized with *italics*. Instructions for how to respond to each item (e.g., check all that apply) appear highlighted in gray.

This survey was developed to be fielded either within the WEOR or within the WOEA.

Administrative Variables

Variables defined in the survey are assumed to be initialized as missing and will be assigned other values only as required for the skip pattern. These are not the analytic variables.

- X date: month, day, and year that is one year before the date the respondent began the survey. Set X date when the respondent answers the consent question, and keep that date no matter when the respondent returns during fielding.

- Harassment: initialize as missing.
- Discrimination: initialize as missing.
- Times: initialize as missing.
- Number: initialize as missing.

Racial/Ethnic Harassment Module

[Do not display module heading to respondents.]

In this section, you will be asked about upsetting or offensive things that someone from [if reservecomp = TRUE, insert here: "your military"] work might have said or done that were related to your race/ethnicity. The questions ask about things that happened *after* [X date]. *Race/Ethnicity* refers to such terms for people as American Indian, Asian, Arab, Black, Filipino, Hispanic, Puerto Rican, Polish, White, and so on. A person can belong to one or more racial/ethnic groups.

When a question mentions "*someone from work*," please include any person you have contact with *as part of your military duties.* "Someone from work" could be a supervisor, a civilian employee, contractor, or military personnel at any rank. They could be in your unit or in other units.

These things might have occurred on duty or off duty, on base or off base. Please include them as long as the person who did them was someone from [if reservecomp = TRUE, insert here: "your military"] work.

[If reservecomp = TRUE, insert here: "Do not include experiences that happened in a nonmilitary job."]

[Programming note: The box below is linked to items H1–H12. Please place the definition box above the question text for all items H1–H12.]

"*Someone from work*" includes any person you have contact with as *part of your military duties.*

Race/Ethnicity refers to such terms for people as American Indian, Asian, Arab, Black, Filipino, Hispanic, Puerto Rican, Polish, White, multiracial, and so on.

H1. **Since** [X date]**, has someone from work made you uncomfortable, angry, or upset by telling racial/ethnic jokes?**

Yes 1

No 2

H2. **Since** [X date]**, has someone from work used a racial/ethnic term that made you uncomfortable, angry, or upset?** For example, an offensive label such as *spic*, *nigger*, *raghead*, *Polack*, or *cracker*.

Yes 1

No 2

H3. **Since** [X date]**, has someone from work made you uncomfortable, angry, or upset by claiming that their race/ethnicity is better than others?**

Yes 1

No 2

H4. **Since** [X date]**, has someone from work made you uncomfortable, angry, or upset by displaying something that threatens or insults a racial/ethnic group?** This includes tattoos, emails, pictures, flags, or anything that insults racial/ethnic groups or refers to racial supremacy groups.

Yes 1

No 2

H5. **Since** [X date]**, has someone from work made you uncomfortable, angry, or upset by insulting your racial/ethnic group?**

Yes 1

No 2

H6. **Since** [X date]**, has someone from work made you uncomfortable, angry, or upset by using a stereotype about your racial/ethnic group?** Stereotypes are beliefs about the characteristics of group members—for example, that they tend to be cheap, aggressive, or shy.

Yes 1

No 2

H7. **Since** [X date]**, has someone from work made you uncomfortable, angry, or upset by making a comment about a physical characteristic of your racial/ethnic group?** This might be, for example, a comment about your skin color, height, hair, or eye shape.

Yes 1

No 2

H8. **Since** [X date]**, has someone from work made you uncomfortable, angry, or upset by making a comment about the way people in your racial/ethnic group talk?**

Yes 1

No 2

H9. **Since** [X date]**, has someone from work made you uncomfortable, angry, or upset by showing you a lack of respect because of your race/ethnicity?**

Yes 1

No 2

H10. **Since** [X date]**, has someone from work made you uncomfortable, angry, or upset by excluding you from an activity because of your race/ethnicity?**

Yes 1

No 2

H11. **Since** [X date]**, has someone from work threatened or physically assaulted you because of your race/ethnicity?**

Yes 1

No 2

[If H11 = 1 (Yes) then Harassment = TRUE.]

H12. We have asked you questions about how someone from work might have created difficulties for you. We are also interested in whether someone from work targeted another person based on their race/ethnicity.

Since [X date]**, has someone from work directed an offensive action or comment at *another person* because of their race/ethnicity?**

Yes 1

No 2

[If H12 = 1 (Yes), continue. Else, skip to H1b.]

H12a. **Did that action or comment make *you* uncomfortable, angry, or upset?**

Yes 1

No 2

[If H1 = 1 (Yes), ask H1b. Else, skip to H2b.]

H1b. You indicated that, after [X date], someone from work made you uncomfortable, angry, or upset by *telling racial/ethnic jokes.*

Do you think they ever knew that you or someone else *wanted them to stop*? If more than one person did this, do you think any of them ever knew?

Yes 1

No 2

[If H1b = 2 (No), skip to H1d.]

H1c. You indicated that, after [X date], someone from work made you uncomfortable, angry, or upset by *telling racial/ethnic jokes.*

Did they *continue* telling these jokes even *after* they knew that you or someone else wanted them to stop?

Yes 1

No 2

[If H1c = 1 (Yes), Harassment = TRUE.]

H1d. You indicated that, after [X date], someone from work made you uncomfortable, angry, or upset by *telling racial/ethnic jokes.*

Do you think most people know that this behavior would be offensive to service members in certain racial/ethnic groups?

Yes 1

No 2

[If H1d = 1 (Yes), then Harassment = TRUE.]

[If H2 = 1 (Yes) ask H2b. Else, skip to H3b.]

H2b. You indicated that, after [X date], someone from work made you uncomfortable, angry, or upset by *using a racial/ethnic term*. For example, an offensive label such as *spic, nigger, raghead, Polack,* or *cracker.*

Do you think they ever knew that you or someone else *wanted them to stop*? If more than one person did this, do you think any of them ever knew?

Yes 1

No 2

[If H2b = 2 (No), skip to H2d.]

H2c. You indicated that, after [X date], someone from work made you uncomfortable, angry, or upset by *using a racial/ethnic term*. For example, an offensive label such as *spic, nigger, raghead, Polack*, or *cracker.*

Did they *continue* using the racial/ethnic term even *after* they knew that you or someone else wanted them to stop?

Yes 1

No 2

[If H2c = 1 (Yes) then Harassment = TRUE.]

H2d. You indicated that, after [X date], someone from work made you uncomfortable, angry, or upset by *using a racial/ethnic term*. For example, an offensive label such as *spic, nigger, raghead, Polack*, or *cracker.*

Do you think most people know that this behavior would be offensive to service members in certain racial/ethnic groups?

Yes 1

No 2

[If H2d = 1 (Yes), Harassment = TRUE.]

[If H3 = 1 (Yes), ask H3b. Else, skip to H4b.]

H3b. You indicated that, after [X date], someone from work made you uncomfortable, angry, or upset by *claiming that their race/ethnicity is better than others.*

Do you think they ever knew that you or someone else *wanted them to stop*? If more than one person did this, do you think any of them ever knew?

Yes 1

No 2

[If H3b = 2 (No), skip to H3d.]

H3c. You indicated that, after [X date], someone from work made you uncomfortable, angry, or upset by *claiming that their race/ethnicity is better than others.*

Did they *continue* making these claims even *after* they knew that you or someone else wanted them to stop?

Yes 1

No 2

[If H3c = 1 (Yes), Harassment = TRUE.]

H3d. You indicated that, after [X date], someone from work made you uncomfortable, angry, or upset by *claiming that their race/ethnicity is better than others.*

Do you think most people know that these claims would be offensive to service members in certain racial/ethnic groups?

Yes 1

No 2

[If H3d = 1 (Yes), Harassment = TRUE.]

[If H4 = 1 (Yes), ask H4b. Else, skip to H5b.]

H4b. You indicated that, after [X date], someone from work made you uncomfortable, angry, or upset by *displaying something that threatens or insults a racial/ethnic group.* This includes tattoos, emails, pictures, flags, and so on.

Do you think they ever knew that you or someone else *wanted them to stop*? If more than one person did this, do you think any of them ever knew?

Yes 1

No 2

[If H4b = 2 (No), skip to H4d.]

H4c. You indicated that, after [X date], someone from work made you uncomfortable, angry, or upset by *displaying something that threatens or insults a racial/ethnic group.* This includes tattoos, emails, pictures, flags, and so on.

Did they *continue* displaying these materials even *after* they knew that you or someone else wanted them to stop?

Yes 1

No 2

[If H4c = 1 (Yes), Harassment = TRUE.]

H4d. You indicated that, after [X date], someone from work made you uncomfortable, angry, or upset by *displaying something that threatens or insults a racial/ethnic group.* This includes tattoos, emails, pictures, flags, and so on.

Do you think most people know that displaying these materials would be offensive to service members in certain racial/ethnic groups?

Yes 1

No 2

[If H4d = 1 (Yes), Harassment = TRUE.]

[If H5 = 1 (Yes), ask H5b. Else, skip to H6b.]

H5b. You indicated that, after [X date], someone from work made you uncomfortable, angry, or upset by *insulting your racial/ethnic group.*

Do you think they ever knew that you or someone else *wanted them to stop*? If more than one person did this, do you think any of them ever knew?

Yes 1

No 2

[If H5b = 2 (No), skip to H5d.]

H5c. You indicated that, after [X date], someone from work made you uncomfortable, angry, or upset by *insulting your racial/ethnic group.*

Did they *continue* these insults even *after* they knew that you or someone else wanted them to stop?

Yes 1

No 2

[If H5c = 1 (Yes), Harassment = TRUE.]

H5d. You indicated that, after [X date], someone from work made you uncomfortable, angry, or upset by *insulting your racial/ethnic group.*

Do you think most people know that these insults would be offensive to service members in certain racial/ethnic groups?

Yes 1

No 2

[If H5d = 1 (Yes), Harassment = TRUE.]

[If H6 = 1 (Yes), ask H6b. Else, skip to H7b.]

H6b. You indicated that, after [X date], someone from work made you uncomfortable, angry, or upset by *using a stereotype about your racial/ethnic group.*

Do you think they ever knew that you or someone else *wanted them to stop*? If more than one person did this, do you think any of them ever knew?

Yes 1

No 2

[If H6b = 2 (No), skip to H6d.]

H6c. You indicated that, after [X date], someone from work made you uncomfortable, angry, or upset by *using a stereotype about your racial/ethnic group.*

Did they *continue* using the stereotype even *after* they knew that you or someone else wanted them to stop?

Yes 1

No 2

[If H6c = 1 (Yes), Harassment = TRUE.]

H6d. You indicated that, after [X date], someone from work made you uncomfortable, angry, or upset by *using a stereotype about your racial/ethnic group.*

Do you think most people know that using this stereotype would be offensive to service members in certain racial/ethnic groups?

Yes 1

No 2

[If H6d = 1 (Yes), Harassment = TRUE.]

[If H7 = 1 (Yes), ask H7b. Else, skip to H8b.]

H7b. You indicated that, after [X date], someone from work made you uncomfortable, angry, or upset by *making a comment about the physical characteristics of your racial/ethnic group.*

Do you think they ever knew that you or someone else *wanted them to stop*? If more than one person did this, do you think any of them ever knew?

Yes 1

No 2

[If H7b = 2 (No), skip to H7d.]

H7c. You indicated that, after [X date], someone from work made you uncomfortable, angry, or upset by *making comments about the physical characteristics of your racial/ethnic group.*

Did they *continue* making these comments even *after* they knew that you or someone else wanted them to stop?

Yes 1

No 2

[If H7c = 1 (Yes), Harassment = TRUE.]

H7d. You indicated that, after [X date], someone from work made you uncomfortable, angry, or upset by *making a comment about the physical characteristics of your racial/ethnic group.*

Do you think most people know that this comment would be offensive to service members in certain racial/ethnic groups?

Yes 1

No 2

[If H7d = 1 (Yes), Harassment = TRUE.]

[If H8 = 1 (Yes), ask H8b. Else, skip to H9b.]

H8b. You indicated that, after [X date], someone from work made you uncomfortable, angry, or upset by *making a comment about the way people in your racial/ethnic group talk.*

Do you think they ever knew that you or someone else *wanted them to stop*? If more than one person did this, do you think any of them ever knew?

Yes 1

No 2

[If H8b = 2 (No), skip to H8d.]

H8c. You indicated that, after [X date], someone from work made you uncomfortable, angry, or upset by *making a comment about the way people in your racial/ethnic group talk.*

Did they *continue* making these comments even *after* they knew that you or someone else wanted them to stop?

Yes 1

No 2

[If H8c = 1 (Yes), Harassment = TRUE.]

H8d. You indicated that, after [X date], someone from work made you uncomfortable, angry, or upset by *making a comment about the way people in your racial/ethnic group talk.*

Do you think most people know that this comment would be offensive to service members in certain racial/ethnic groups?

Yes 1

No 2

[If H8d = 1 (Yes), Harassment = TRUE.]

[If H9 = 1 (Yes), ask H9b. Else, skip to H10b.]

H9b. You indicated that, after [X date], someone from work made you uncomfortable, angry, or upset by *showing you a lack of respect because of your race/ethnicity.*

Do you think they ever knew that you or someone else *wanted them to stop*? If more than one person did this, do you think any of them ever knew?

Yes 1

No 2

[If H9b = 2 (No), skip to H9d.]

H9c. You indicated that, after [X date], someone from work made you uncomfortable, angry, or upset by *showing you a lack of respect because of your race/ethnicity.*

Did they *continue* showing a lack of respect even *after* they knew that you or someone else wanted them to stop?

Yes 1

No 2

[If H9c = 1 (Yes), Harassment = TRUE.]

H9d. You indicated that, after [X date], someone from work made you uncomfortable, angry, or upset by *showing you a lack of respect because of your race/ethnicity.*

Do you think most people know that this behavior would be offensive to service members in certain racial/ethnic groups?

Yes 1

No 2

[If H9d = 1 (Yes), Harassment = TRUE.]

[If H10 = 1 (Yes), ask H10b. Else, skip to H12b.]

H10b. You indicated that, after [X date], someone from work made you uncomfortable, angry, or upset by *excluding you from an activity because of your race/ethnicity.*

Do you think they ever knew that you or someone else *wanted them to stop*? If more than one person did this, do you think any of them ever knew?

Yes 1

No 2

[If H10b = 2 (No), skip to H10d.]

H10c. You indicated that, after [X date], someone from work made you uncomfortable, angry, or upset by *excluding you from an activity because of your race/ethnicity.*

Did they *continue* excluding you even *after* they knew that you or someone else wanted them to stop?

Yes 1

No 2

[If H10c = 1 (Yes), Harassment = TRUE.]

H10d. You indicated that, after [X date], someone from work made you uncomfortable, angry, or upset by *excluding you from an activity because of your race/ethnicity.*

Do you think most people know that this behavior would be offensive to service members in certain racial/ethnic groups?

Yes 1

No 2

[If H10d = 1 (Yes), Harassment = TRUE.]

[If H12a = 1 (Yes), ask H12b. Else, skip to RH_F1.]

H12b. You indicated that, after [X date], someone from work made you uncomfortable, angry, or upset by *directing an offensive action or comment at another person because of their race/ethnicity.*

Do you think they ever knew that you or someone else *wanted them to stop*? If more than one person did this, do you think any of them ever knew?

Yes 1

No 2

[If H12b = 2 (No), skip to H12d.]

H12c. You indicated that, after [X date], someone from work made you uncomfortable, angry, or upset by *directing an offensive action or comment at another person because of their race/ethnicity.*

Did they *continue* the offensive actions or comments even after they knew that you or someone else wanted them to stop?

Yes 1

No 2

[If H12c = 1 (Yes), Harassment = TRUE.]

H12d. You indicated that, after [X date], someone from work made you uncomfortable, angry, or upset by *directing an offensive action or comment at another person because of their race/ethnicity.*

Do you think most people know that the action or comment would be offensive to many service members?

Yes 1

No 2

[If H12d = 1 (Yes), Harassment = TRUE.]

[If any (H1 to H11 = 1 (Yes) OR H12a = 1 (Yes)), ask RH_F1. Else, skip to RD1.]

RH_F1. Earlier you answered questions about upsetting things that someone from work did since [X date]. **Do you consider any of the things you experienced to be racial/ethnic harassment?**

Yes 1

No 2

[If any (H1c, H1d, H2c, H2d, H3c, H3d, H4c, H4d, H12c, or H12d) = 1 (Yes), ask RH_F2. Else, skip to RD1.]

RH_F2. The next question will ask about some of your experiences. Please consider the following things that someone from work did:

- Told racial/ethnic jokes [display if H1c = 1 (Yes) or H1d = 1 (Yes)]
- Used an offensive racial/ethnic term [display if H2c = 1 (Yes) or H2d = 1 (Yes)]
- Claimed that their race/ethnicity is better than others [display if H3c = 1 (Yes) or H3d = 1 (Yes)]
- Displayed something that threatens or insults a racial/ethnic group [display if H4c = 1 (Yes) or H4d = 1 (Yes)]
- Directed an offensive action or comment at another person because of their race/ethnicity [display if H12c = 1 (Yes) or H12d = 1 (Yes)]

Thinking about the workplace experiences that upset you, was the upsetting behavior directed at . . .

Your racial/ethnic group? 1
Someone else's racial/ethnic group? 2
Both your racial/ethnic group and another racial/ethnic group? 3

Racial/Ethnic Discrimination Module

[Do not display module heading to respondents.]

The next questions ask if someone from work treated you unfairly because of your race/ethnicity and if they would have treated someone of a different race/ethnicity better.

RD1. **Since [X date], did someone give you a lower military performance evaluation because of your race/ethnicity?**

Yes 1
No 2

[If RD1 = 1 (Yes), continue. Else, skip to RD2.]

What led you to believe that the person gave you a lower military performance evaluation because of your race/ethnicity? Select all that apply.

RD1b. The person made a comment showing they took your race/ethnicity into account.	Yes 1	No 2
RD1c. The person said or did something showing they dislike your racial/ethnic group.	Yes 1	No 2
RD1d. The person treated you worse than other people in the same situation who were of a different race/ethnicity.	Yes 1	No 2
RD1e. You suspect it was due to your race/ethnicity because it is common for people in the military to mistreat people of your race/ethnicity.	Yes 1	No 2

[If RD1b = 1 or RD1c = 1 or RD1d = 1, Discrimination = TRUE.]

RD2. **Since** [X date]**, did someone make it harder for you to get a military award because of your race/ethnicity?** This includes ribbons, medals, coins, quarterly or annual awards, decorations, and commendations.

Yes 1

No 2

[If RD2 = 1 (Yes), continue. Else, skip to RD3.]

What led you to believe that the person made it harder for you to get a military award because of your race/ethnicity? Select all that apply.

RD2b. The person made a comment showing they took your race/ethnicity into account.	Yes 1	No 2
RD2c. The person said or did something showing they dislike your racial/ethnic group.	Yes 1	No 2
RD2d. The person treated you worse than other people in the same situation who were of a different race/ethnicity.	Yes 1	No 2
RD2e. You suspect it was due to your race/ethnicity because it is common for people in the military to mistreat people of your race/ethnicity.	Yes 1	No 2

[If RD2b = 1 (Yes) or RD2c = 1 (Yes) or RD2d = 1 (Yes), Discrimination = TRUE.]

RD3. **Since** [X date]**, did someone make it harder for you to get a military promotion because of your race/ethnicity?**

Yes 1

No 2

[If RD3 = 1 (yes), continue. Else, skip to RD4.]

What led you to believe that the person made it harder for you to get a military promotion because of your race/ethnicity? Select all that apply.

RD3b. The person made a comment showing they took your race/ethnicity into account.	Yes 1	No 2
RD3c. The person said or did something showing that they dislike your racial/ethnic group.	Yes 1	No 2
RD3d. The person treated you worse than other people in the same situation who were of a different race/ethnicity.	Yes 1	No 2
RD3e. You suspect it was due to your race/ethnicity because it is common for people in the military to mistreat people of your race/ethnicity.	Yes 1	No 2

[If RD3b = 1 (Yes) or RD3c = 1 (Yes) or RD3d = 1 (Yes), Discrimination = TRUE.]

RD4. **Since** [X date]**, did someone from the military make it difficult or impossible for you to go into your preferred military occupation because of your race/ethnicity?** For example, your preferred MOS, career field, [Air Force specialty code], or rating.

Yes 1

No 2

[If RD4 = 1 (Yes), continue. Else, skip to RD5.]

What led you to believe that the person made it difficult or impossible for you to go into your preferred military occupation because of your race/ethnicity? Select all that apply.

RD4b. The person made a comment showing they took your race/ethnicity into account.	Yes 1	No 2
RD4c. The person said or did something showing that they dislike your racial/ethnic group.	Yes 1	No 2
RD4d. The person treated you worse than other people in the same situation who were of a different race/ethnicity.	Yes 1	No 2
RD4e. You suspect it was due to your race/ethnicity because it is common for people in the military to mistreat people of your race/ethnicity.	Yes 1	No 2

[If RD4b = 1 (Yes) or RD4c = 1 (Yes) or RD4d = 1 (Yes), Discrimination = TRUE.]

RD5. **Since** [X date]**, did someone assign you to an undesirable military unit, installation, or country because of your race/ethnicity?**

Yes 1

No 2

[If RD5 = 1 (Yes), continue. Else, skip to RD6.]

What led you to believe that the person assigned you to an undesirable military unit, installation, or country because of your race/ethnicity? Select all that apply.

RD5b. The person made a comment showing they took your race/ethnicity into account.	Yes 1	No 2
RD5c. The person said or did something showing that they dislike your racial/ethnic group.	Yes 1	No 2
RD5d. The person treated you worse than other people in the same situation who were of a different race/ethnicity.	Yes 1	No 2
RD5e. You suspect it was due to your race/ethnicity because it is common for people in the military to mistreat people of your race/ethnicity.	Yes 1	No 2

[If RD5b = 1 (Yes) or RD5c = 1 (Yes) or RD5d = 1 (Yes), Discrimination = TRUE.]

RD6. **Since** [X date]**, did someone assign you to either an undesirable or unimportant military task because of your race/ethnicity?**

Yes 1

No 2

[If RD6 = 1 (Yes), continue. Else, skip to RD7.]

What led you to believe that the person assigned you to either an undesirable or unimportant military task because of your race/ethnicity? Select all that apply.

RD6b. The person made a comment showing they took your race/ethnicity into account.	Yes 1	No 2
RD6c. The person said or did something showing that they dislike your racial/ethnic group.	Yes 1	No 2
RD6d. The person treated you worse than other people in the same situation who were of a different race/ethnicity.	Yes 1	No 2
RD6e. You suspect it was due to your race/ethnicity because it is common for people in the military to mistreat people of your race/ethnicity.	Yes 1	No 2

[If RD6b = 1 (Yes) or RD6c = 1 (Yes) or RD6d = 1 (Yes), Discrimination = TRUE.]

RD7. **Since** [X date]**, did someone make it difficult or impossible for you to get a military training opportunity because of your race/ethnicity?**

Yes 1

No 2

[If RD7 = 1 (Yes), continue. Else, skip to RD8.]

What led you to believe that the person made it difficult or impossible for you to get a military training opportunity because of your race/ethnicity? Select all that apply.

RD7b. The person made a comment showing they took your race/ethnicity into account.	Yes 1	No 2
RD7c. The person said or did something showing that they dislike your racial/ethnic group.	Yes 1	No 2
RD7d. The person treated you worse than other people in the same situation who were of a different race/ethnicity.	Yes 1	No 2
RD7e. You suspect it was due to your race/ethnicity because it is common for people in the military to mistreat people of your race/ethnicity.	Yes 1	No 2

[If RD7b = 1 (Yes) or RD7c = 1 (Yes) or RD7d = 1 (Yes), Discrimination = TRUE.]

RD8. **Since** [X date], **did someone give you an unfair military training evaluation or grade because of your race/ethnicity?**

Yes 1

No 2

[If RD8 = 1 (Yes), continue. Else, skip to RD9.]

What led you to believe that the person gave you an unfair military training evaluation or grade because of your race/ethnicity? Select all that apply.

RD8b. The person made a comment showing they took your race/ethnicity into account.	Yes 1	No 2
RD8c. The person said or did something showing that they dislike your racial/ethnic group.	Yes 1	No 2
RD8d. The person treated you worse than other people in the same situation who were of a different race/ethnicity.	Yes 1	No 2
RD8e. You suspect it was due to your race/ethnicity because it is common for people in the military to mistreat people of your race/ethnicity.	Yes 1	No 2

[If RD8b = 1 (Yes) or RD8c = 1 (Yes) or RD8d = 1 (Yes), Discrimination = TRUE.]

RD9. **Since** [X date], **did someone deny your military leave, pass, or liberty request because of your race/ethnicity?**

Yes 1

No 2

[If RD9 = 1 (Yes), continue. Else, skip to RD10.]

What led you to believe that the person denied your military leave, pass, or liberty request because of your race/ethnicity? Select all that apply.

RD9b. The person made a comment showing they took your race/ethnicity into account.	Yes 1	No 2
RD9c. The person said or did something showing that they dislike your racial/ethnic group.	Yes 1	No 2
RD9d. The person treated you worse than other people in the same situation who were of a different race/ethnicity.	Yes 1	No 2
RD9e. You suspect it was due to your race/ethnicity because it is common for people in the military to mistreat people of your race/ethnicity.	Yes 1	No 2

[If RD9b = 1 (Yes) or RD9c = 1 (Yes) or RD9d = 1 (Yes), Discrimination = TRUE.]

RD10. **Since** [X date]**, did someone from the military punish you unfairly because of your race/ethnicity?** For example, you were disciplined more harshly for misconduct than someone of another race/ethnicity.

Yes 1

No 2

[If RD10 = 1 (Yes), continue. Else, skip to RD11.]

What led you to believe that the person punished you unfairly because of your race/ethnicity? Select all that apply.

RD10b. The person made a comment showing they took your race/ethnicity into account.	Yes 1	No 2
RD10c. The person said or did something showing that they dislike your racial/ethnic group.	Yes 1	No 2
RD10d. The person treated you worse than other people in the same situation who were of a different race/ethnicity.	Yes 1	No 2
RD10e. You suspect it was due to your race/ethnicity because it is common for people in the military to mistreat people of your race/ethnicity.	Yes 1	No 2

[If RD10b = 1 (Yes) or RD10c = 1 (Yes) or RD10d = 1 (Yes), Discrimination = TRUE.]

RD11. The military provides many types of services and benefits to service members, such as health care, military housing, recreation centers, commissaries, military law enforcement, and other services.

Since [X date]**, did someone in one of these jobs provide worse service or fewer benefits to you because of your race/ethnicity?**

Yes 1

No 2

[If RD11 = 1 (Yes), continue. Else, skip to RD12.]

What led you to believe that the person provided worse service or fewer benefits to you because of your race/ethnicity? Select all that apply.

RD11b. The person made a comment showing they took your race/ethnicity into account.	Yes 1	No 2
RD11c. The person said or did something showing that they dislike your racial/ethnic group.	Yes 1	No 2
RD11d. The person treated you worse than other people in the same situation who were of a different race/ethnicity.	Yes 1	No 2
RD11e. You suspect it was due to your race/ethnicity because it is common for people in the military to mistreat people of your race/ethnicity.	Yes 1	No 2

[If RD11b = 1 (Yes) or RD11c = 1 (Yes) or RD11d = 1 (Yes), Discrimination = TRUE.]

[If reservecomp = TRUE, ask RD12. Else, skip to RD_F1.]

RD12. **Since** [X date]**, did someone from the military restrict your options for scheduling your military requirements because of your race/ethnicity?** For example, scheduling drill days or military training.

Yes 1

No 2

[If RD12 = 1 (Yes), continue. Else, skip to RD_F1.]

What led you to believe that the person restricted your options for scheduling your military requirements because of your race/ethnicity? Select all that apply.

RD12b. The person made a comment showing they took your race/ethnicity into account.	Yes 1	No 2
RD12c. The person said or did something showing that they dislike your racial/ethnic group.	Yes 1	No 2
RD12d. The person treated you worse than other people in the same situation who were of a different race/ethnicity.	Yes 1	No 2
RD12e. You suspect it was due to your race/ethnicity because it is common for people in the military to mistreat people of your race/ethnicity.	Yes 1	No 2

[If RD12b = 1 (Yes) or RD12c = 1 (Yes) or RD12d = 1 (Yes), Discrimination = TRUE.]

[If any RD1 to RD12 = 1 (Yes), continue. Else skip to F1.]

RD_F1. Earlier you answered questions about unfair things that someone from work has done since [X date]. **Do you consider any of the things that happened to you to be racial/ethnic discrimination?**

Yes 1

No 2

Module to Assess the Characteristics of the Offender(s) and Situation, Reporting Decisions, System Response, and Barriers to Reporting

[Do not display module heading to respondents.]

[If (Harassment = TRUE) or (Discrimination = TRUE), continue. Else, skip past the remainder of RAND-designed survey.]

F1. Based on your answers earlier, it appears that, in the last 12 months, at least one person acted in a way that created an upsetting or unfair work environment.

The next questions will ask for additional information about some of those experiences. Please consider the following things that someone from work did:

- Told racial/ethnic jokes [display if H1c = 1 (yes) or H1d = 1 (yes)]
- Used an offensive racial/ethnic term [display if H2c = 1 (yes) or H2d = 1 (yes)]
- Claimed that their race/ethnicity is better than others [display if H3c = 1 (yes) or H3d = 1 (yes)]
- Displayed something that threatens or insults a racial/ethnic group [display if H4c = 1 (yes) or H4d = 1 (yes)]
- Insulted your racial/ethnic group [display if H5c = 1 (yes) or H5d = 1 (yes)]
- Used a stereotype about your racial/ethnic group [display if H6c = 1 (yes) or H6d = 1 (yes)]
- Made a comment about a physical characteristic of your racial/ethnic group [display if H7c = 1 (yes) or H7d = 1 (yes)]
- Made a comment about the way people in your racial/ethnic group talk [display if H8c = 1 (yes) or H8d = 1 (yes)]
- Showed you a lack of respect because of your race/ethnicity [display if H9c = 1 (yes) or H9d = 1 (yes)]
- Excluded you from an activity because of your race/ethnicity [display if H10c = 1 (yes) or H10d = 1 (yes)]
- Threatened or physically assaulted you because of your race/ethnicity [display if H11 = 1 (yes)]
- Directed an offensive action or comment at *someone else* because of their race/ethnicity [display if H12c = 1 (yes) or H12d = 1 (yes)]
- Gave you a lower military performance evaluation because of your race/ ethnicity [display if RD1b = 1 (yes) or RD1c = 1 (yes) or RD1d = 1 (yes)]
- Made it harder for you to get a military award because of your race/ ethnicity [display if RD2b = 1 (yes) or RD2c = 1 (yes) or RD2d = 1 (yes)]

- Made it harder for you to get a military promotion because of your race/ ethnicity [display if RD3b = 1 (yes) or RD3c = 1 (yes) or RD3d = 1 (yes)]
- Made it difficult or impossible for you to go into your preferred military occupation because of your race/ethnicity [display if RD4b = 1 (yes) or RD4c = 1 (yes) or RD4d = 1 (yes)]
- Assigned you to an undesirable military unit, installation, or country because of your race/ethnicity [display if RD5b = 1 (yes) or RD5c = 1 (yes) or RD5d = 1 (yes)]
- Assigned you to either an undesirable or unimportant military task because of your race/ethnicity [display if RD6b = 1 (yes) or RD6c = 1 (yes) or RD6d = 1 (yes)]
- Made it difficult or impossible for you to get a military training opportunity because of your race/ethnicity [display if RD7b = 1 (yes) or RD7c = 1 (yes) or RD7d = 1 (yes)]
- Gave you an unfair military training evaluation or grade because of your race/ethnicity [display if RD8b = 1 (yes) or RD8c = 1 (yes) or RD8d = 1 (yes)]
- Denied your military leave, pass, or liberty request because of your race/ ethnicity [display if RD9b = 1 (yes) or RD9c = 1 (yes) or RD9d = 1 (yes)]
- Punished you unfairly because of your race/ethnicity [display if RD10b = 1 (yes) or RD10c = 1 (yes) or RD10d = 1 (yes)]
- Provided worse service or fewer benefits to you because of your race/ ethnicity [display if RD11b = 1 (yes) or RD11c = 1 (yes) or RD11d = 1 (yes)]
- Restricted your options for scheduling your military requirements because of your race/ethnicity [display if RD12b = 1 (yes) or RD12c = 1 (yes) or RD12d = 1 (yes)]

Thinking about these upsetting or unfair experiences, were *all* of the behaviors since [X date] **done by *one person*?**

Yes 1

No 2

[If F1 = 1 (Yes), then number = "ind" and skip to F4. Else continue.]

F2. **Were all of the behaviors since** [X date] **done by one group of people who worked or hung out together?** For example, people in the same military unit or a group of friends.

Yes 1

No 2

[If F2 = 1 (Yes), then number = "grp" and skip to F4. Else continue.]

F3. You indicated that you had more than one situation that involved upsetting or unfair behavior since [X date]. Each situation involved either one person or a group of people working together.

For the next series of questions, we will ask about one upsetting or unfair situation. For the next questions, please think about the *one situation* since [X date] that you consider to be *the worst or the most serious.*

In the *worst or most serious situation*, were the upsetting or unfair behaviors done by . . .

One individual? 1

A group of individuals working together? 2

[If F3 = 1 (One individual), then number = "ind." Else number = "grp"]

F4. **Thinking about the situation, about how long did the upsetting or unfair behaviors continue?** The situation might have started even before [X date]. If the situation is still happening, indicate how long it has been going on. Select one.

One day 1

2–6 days 2

1–4 weeks 3

1–11 months 4

12 months or more 5

[If number = "grp," skip to F10. Else continue.]

F5. **Was the person who did this . . .** Select one or more. [Program as a checklist rather than as yes/no boxes for each.]

American Indian or Alaska Native? 1

Asian? 2

Black or African American? 3

Hispanic or Latino? 4

Native Hawaiian or other Pacific Islander? 5

White? 6

Other? 7

I don't know their race/ethnicity 97

F6. **Was the person who did this a . . .**

Man? 1

Woman? 2

F7. **Was the person who did this . . .** Select one.

One of your work supervisors or unit leaders? 1

One of your peers at about the same level? 2

One of your subordinates or someone you managed? 3

F8. **Was the person who did this . . .** Select one.

A service member of higher rank than you? 1

A service member of the same rank as you? 2

A service member of lower rank than you? 3

A civilian/contractor working for the military? 4

Do not know 97

[If F8 = (1 or 2 or 3), continue. Else, skip to F15.]

F9. **What was the pay grade of the person who did this?** Select one.

E1–E4 1

E5–E9 2

W1–W5 3

O1–O3 4

O4–O10 5

I don't know their pay grade 97

[Skip to F15.]

F10. **Were any of the people who did this . . .** Select all that apply.

F10a. American Indian or Alaska Native?	Yes 1	No 2
F10b. Asian?	Yes 1	No 2
F10c. Black or African American?	Yes 1	No 2
F10d. Hispanic or Latino?	Yes 1	No 2
F10e. Native Hawaiian or other Pacific Islander?	Yes 1	No 2
F10f. White?	Yes 1	No 2
F10g. Other?	Yes 1	No 2
F10h. Do not know	Yes 1	No 2

F11. **Were the people who did this . . .** Select one.

Men? 1

Women? 2

A mix of men and women? 3

F12. **Were any of the people who did this . . .** Select all that apply.

F12a. One of your work supervisors or unit leaders?	Yes 1	No 2
F12b. One of your peers at about the same level?	Yes 1	No 2
F12c. One of your subordinates or someone you managed?	Yes 1	No 2

F13. **Were any of the people who did this . . .** Select all that apply.

F13a. Service members of higher rank than you?	Yes 1	No 2	Do not know 97
F13b. Service members of about the same rank as you?	Yes 1	No 2	Do not know 97
F13c. Service members of lower rank than you?	Yes 1	No 2	Do not know 97
F13d. Civilians/contractors working for the military?	Yes 1	No 2	Do not know 97

[If F13a = 1 (Yes) or F13b = 1 (Yes) or F13c = 1 (Yes), continue. Else, skip to F15.]

F14. **Were any of the people who did this . . .** Select all that apply.

F14a. E1–E4?	Yes 1	No 2	Do not know 97
F14b. E5–E9?	Yes 1	No 2	Do not know 97
F14c. W1–W5?	Yes 1	No 2	Do not know 97
F14d. O1–O3?	Yes 1	No 2	Do not know 97
F14e. O4–O10?	Yes 1	No 2	Do not know 97

F15. **Thinking about this upsetting or unfair situation . . .**

F15a. Did it ever occur on a military installation or ship [If reservecomp = TRUE, insert here: ", armory, or Reserve unit site"]?	Yes 1	No 2
F15b. Did it ever occur while you were on [temporary duty]/[temporary additional duty], at sea, or during field exercises or alerts?	Yes 1	No 2
F15c. Did it ever occur while you were deployed to a combat zone or to an area where you drew imminent danger pay or hostile fire pay?	Yes 1	No 2
F15d. Did it ever occur during recruit training or basic training?	Yes 1	No 2
F15e. Did it ever occur in a nonmilitary setting? For example, off base or off post.	Yes 1	No 2
F15f. Did it ever occur on duty?	Yes 1	No 2

F16. **Thinking about this upsetting or unfair situation . . .**

F16a. Did you request a transfer or other change of assignment as a result of the situation?	Yes 1	No 2
F16b. Did this situation make you want to leave the military?	Yes 1	No 2
F16c. Did this situation ever make it hard to do your job or complete your work?	Yes 1	No 2
F16d. Did this situation ever make your workplace less productive or compromise your unit's mission?	Yes 1	No 2
F16e. Did you take a sick call day or any other type of leave because of this situation?	Yes 1	No 2
F16f. Did this situation either cause arguments in the workplace or reduce unit cohesion?	Yes 1	No 2
F16g. Did this situation damage your relationships with coworkers?	Yes 1	No 2

F17. **Thinking about this upsetting or unfair situation . . .**

F17a. Did this situation damage your personal relationships with friends or family?	Yes 1	No 2
F17b. Did this situation make you feel down, depressed, or hopeless?	Yes 1	No 2
F17c. Did this situation make you angry?	Yes 1	No 2
F17d. Did this situation make you nervous or stressed?	Yes 1	No 2
F17e. Did this situation make you on guard, watchful, or easily startled?	Yes 1	No 2
F17f. Did this situation make you have trouble sleeping or give you nightmares?	Yes 1	No 2

F18. **Thinking about this upsetting or unfair situation . . .**

F18a. Did you discuss this situation with your friends or family?	Yes 1	No 2
F18b. Did you discuss this situation with a military coworker, chaplain, or counselor?	Yes 1	No 2
F18c. Did you discuss this situation with the person(s) who did the upsetting or unfair things?	Yes 1	No 2
F18d. Did you discuss this situation with a work supervisor or anyone up the chain of command?	Yes 1	No 2
F18e. Did you discuss this situation with any other person tasked with addressing harassment or discrimination in the military?	Yes 1	No 2

[IF F18d = 1 (Yes) OR F18e = 1 (Yes) continue. Else skip to F22.]

F19. You discussed the situation with a person who can handle Military Equal Opportunity (MEO) complaints, including harassment or discrimination. That person might have filed an official report of an MEO violation. You might have met with a military investigator or mediator to describe the harassment or discrimination, for example, an Equal Opportunity Specialist or Equal Opportunity Officer.

Do you believe that someone made an official report of a Military Equal Opportunity (MEO) violation about this situation?

Yes 1
No 2

F20. **What actions were taken in response to you** [if F19 = 1 (Yes), display: "reporting the situation"; else, display "discussing the situation with a supervisor or military official"]**?**

F20a. No action was taken because you asked for the discussion to be kept private.	Yes 1	No 2	Do not know 97
F20b. No action was taken because you chose not to give enough details about the situation.	Yes 1	No 2	Do not know 97
F20c. No action was taken because the person did not believe that it happened.	Yes 1	No 2	Do not know 97
F20d. No action was taken because the person you told decided not to do anything.	Yes 1	No 2	Do not know 97
F20e. You were encouraged to ask the [if number = "ind," display "person"; else, display "people"] to change their upsetting or offensive behavior.	Yes 1	No 2	Do not know 97
F20f. Someone talked to the [if number = "ind," display "person"; else, display "people"] to ask them to change their behavior.	Yes 1	No 2	Do not know 97
F20g. The rules on harassment or discrimination were explained to everyone in the workplace.	Yes 1	No 2	Do not know 97
F20h. Your workstation or duties were changed to help you avoid [if number = "ind," display "that person"; else, display "those people"].	Yes 1	No 2	Do not know 97
F20i. The [if number = "ind," display "person was"; else, display "people were"] moved or reassigned so that you did not have as much contact with them.	Yes 1	No 2	Do not know 97
F20j. There was some official career action taken against the [if number = "ind," display "person"; else, display "people"] for their upsetting behavior (for example, a negative evaluation or fitness report).	Yes 1	No 2	Do not know 97
F20k. You were encouraged to drop the issue.	Yes 1	No 2	Do not know 97
F20l. You were discouraged from filing a formal complaint.	Yes 1	No 2	Do not know 97
F20m. Your coworkers treated you worse, avoided you, or blamed you for the problem.	Yes 1	No 2	Do not know 97
F20n. Your supervisor punished you for bringing it up (for example, loss of privileges, denied promotion, or transferred to a less favorable job).	Yes 1	No 2	Do not know 97

F21. **How satisfied are you with the following aspects of how the discussion or report was handled?** Select one answer for each item.

F21a. Availability of information about how to file an official MEO complaint	Very dissatisfied 1	Dissatisfied 2	Neither dissatisfied nor satisfied 3	Satisfied 4	Very satisfied 5
F21b. How you were treated by the personnel handling your situation	Very dissatisfied 1	Dissatisfied 2	Neither dissatisfied nor satisfied 3	Satisfied 4	Very satisfied 5
F21c. The action taken to stop the problem by the personnel handling your situation	Very dissatisfied 1	Dissatisfied 2	Neither dissatisfied nor satisfied 3	Satisfied 4	Very satisfied 5
F21d. The current status of the situation	Very dissatisfied 1	Dissatisfied 2	Neither dissatisfied nor satisfied 3	Satisfied 4	Very satisfied 5
F21e. Amount of time it took to address your situation	Very dissatisfied 1	Dissatisfied 2	Neither dissatisfied nor satisfied 3	Satisfied 4	Very satisfied 5
F21f. Availability of information or updates on the status of your report or complaint	Very dissatisfied 1	Dissatisfied 2	Neither dissatisfied nor satisfied 3	Satisfied 4	Very satisfied 5

[Skip to F24]

F22. **What were your reasons for not discussing the situation with someone who is responsible for stopping these types of upsetting or unfair behaviors?** These people include your supervisor, someone above you in your chain of command, or a person who enforces equal opportunity regulations. Select all the reasons that apply to you. [Program as a checklist rather than as yes/no boxes for each.]

F22a. The offensive behavior stopped on its own.

F22b. Someone else already reported it.

F22c. Someone told you not to report it.

F22d. You thought it was not serious enough to report.

F22e. You wanted to forget about it or move on.

F22f. You did not know how to report it.

F22g. You did not think anything would be done.

F22h. You did not think you would be believed.

F22i. You did not trust that the process would be fair.

F22j. You thought other people would blame you for the situation.

F22k. You thought you might get in trouble for something you did.

F22l. You thought a supervisor would make too big a deal out of it.

F22m. You thought you might be labeled as a troublemaker.

F22n. You thought it might hurt your performance evaluation or fitness report.

F22o. You thought it might hurt your career.

F22p. You did not want to hurt the person's career.

F22q. You were worried about retaliation by the person(s) who did it.

F22r. You were worried about retaliation by a supervisor or someone in your chain of command.

F22s. You were worried about retaliation by your military coworkers or peers.

F22t. You did not want people to see you as weak.

F22u. You would have felt embarrassed to report it.

F22v. Reporting it would harm your unit's performance or cohesion.

F22w. You took other actions to handle the situation.

[If more than one response F22a–F22w is selected, continue. Else, skip to F24.]

F23. **Which was your main reason for not discussing the situation with someone who is responsible for stopping these types of upsetting or unfair behaviors?** Select one.

[Display all endorsed probes from F22a–F22w.]

F24. **As of today,** [if number = "ind," display "has the person"; else, display "have the people"] **stopped their upsetting or unfair behavior?**

Yes 1

No 2

Derived Variable Definitions

The pseudocode given here provides suggestions for derived variables to be included in reports on racial/ethnic harassment and discrimination based on the survey questions in Appendix A. It was written without access to a completed data set and, as such, has not been debugged. Users should view these variable definitions as suggestions that require formalization into their preferred programming language followed by careful stress testing to ensure accuracy.

MEO_HX are new derived variables that code the final classification of the series of harassment questions H1 to H12a.

For example, MEO_H1 is a (1, 0, missing1, missing2, missing3) variable that corresponds to the series H1 → H1b → H1c → H1d.

Definitions assume that 1 = YES, 2 = NO, –5 = Respondent skipped

Each derived MEO_HX variable is based on a single series of questions, starting with a broad gateway/screener question that is followed by items that apply additional definitional criteria. General rules for coding derived MEO_H variables are the following:

1. If the respondent answers "no" to a gateway question, they are classified as not experiencing that type of event.
2. If the respondent chooses to skip a gateway question, they are classified as missing on that type of event.
3. If the respondent answers "yes" to a gateway question, and "yes" to enough follow-ups to meet our definitional criteria in one way, they are coded as experiencing that type of event regardless of how many other follow-up items they skipped.
4. If the respondent answers "yes" to a gateway question, skips fewer than half of the follow-up criteria questions, and responds "no" to

those follow-ups they did answer, they are coded as not experiencing that type of event.

5. If the respondent answers "yes" to a gateway question and skips half or more of the follow-ups, they are coded as missing.

Definitions for MEO_H1 to MEO_H10

/* initialize new variable with all missing values */
Set MEO_H1 to **tempmissing**
/* MEO_HX is missing type 1 if the respondent skipped the gate question */
Set MEO_H1 to **missing1** IF (H1 = **–5**)
/* MEO_HX is missing type 2 if the respondent skipped both the persistence and severity criterion */
Set MEO_H1 to **missing2** IF (H1 = **1** AND H1c = **–5** AND H1d = **–5**)
/* MEO_HX is missing type 3 if the respondent skipped either the persistence or the severity criterion */
Set MEO_1 to **missing3** IF (H1 = **1** AND (H1c = **–5** OR H1d = **–5**))
/* MEO_HX occurred if the respondent indicates "yes" to the gate question, and "yes" to either the persistence or severity criterion */
Set MEO_H1 to **1** IF (H1 = **1** AND (H1c = **1** OR H1d = **1**))
/* MEO_HX did not occur if the respondent indicates "no" to the gate question, or "no" to both the persistence and severity criteria */
Set MEO_H1 to **0** IF (H1 = **2** OR ((H1b = **2** OR H1c = **2**) AND H1d = **2**))

Definitions for MEO_H11

/* initialize new variable with all missing values */
Set MEO_H11 to **tempmissing**
/* MEO_H11 is missing type 1 if the respondent skipped the gate question */
Set MEO_H11 to **missing1** IF (H11 = **–5**)
/* MEO_H11 occurred if the respondent indicates "yes" to the gate question */
Set MEO_H11 to **1** IF (H11 = **1**)
/* MEO_H11 did not occur if the respondent indicates "no" to the gate question */
Set MEO_H11 to **0** IF (H11 = **2**)

Definitions for MEO_H12

/* initialize new variable with all missing values */

Set MEO_H12 to **tempmissing**

/* MEO_H12 is missing type 1 if the respondent skipped the gate question or the follow-up to the gate question */

Set MEO_H12 to **missing1** IF (H12 = **–5** OR H12a = **–5**)

/* MEO_H12 is missing type 2 if the respondent skipped both the persistence and severity criteria */

Set MEO_H12 to **missing2** IF (H12a = **1** AND H12c = **–5** AND H12d = **–5**)

/* MEO_H12 is missing type 3 if the respondent skipped either the persistence or the severity criterion but not both*/

Set MEO_H12 to **missing3** IF (H12a = **1** AND (H12c = **–5** OR H12d = **–5**))

/* MEO_H12 occurred if the respondent indicates "yes" to the follow-up to the gating question, and "yes" to either the persistence or severity criterion */

Set MEO_H12 to **1** IF (H12a = **1** AND (H12c = **1** OR H12d = **1**))

/* MEO_H12 did not occur if the respondent indicates "no" to the gate question, "no" to the follow-up to the gating question, or "no" to both the persistence and severity criteria */

Set MEO_H12 to **0** IF (H12 = **2** OR H12a = **2** OR ((H12b = **2** OR H12c = **2**) AND H12d = **2**))

MEO_D*X* are new derived variables that code the final classification of the series of discrimination questions RD1 to RD11.

For example, MEO_D1 is a (1, 0, missing1, missing4) variable that corresponds to the series RD1 → RD1b–RD1e.

Definitions assume that 1 = YES, 2 = NO, –5 = Respondent skipped

Each derived MEO_D*X* variable is based on a single series of questions, starting with a broad gateway/screener question that is followed by items that apply additional definitional criteria. General rules for coding derived MEO_D*X* variables are as follows:

1. If the respondent answers "no" to a gateway question, they are classified as not experiencing that type of event.

2. If the respondent chooses to skip a gateway question, they are classified as missing on that type of event.
3. If the respondent answers "yes" to a gateway question, and "yes" to either RDXb, RDXc, or RDXd, they meet definitional criteria and are coded as experiencing that type of event regardless of how many other follow-up items they skipped.
4. If the respondent answers "yes" to a gateway question, skips no more than one item RDXb–RDXd, and responds "no" to those follow-ups they did answer, they are coded as not experiencing that type of event.
5. If the respondent answers "yes" to a gateway question and skips half or more of the diagnostic follow-ups (RDXb–RDXd), they are coded as missing.

Definitions for MEO_D1 to MEO_D12

/* initialize new variable with all missing values */

Set MEO_D1 to **tempmissing**

/* MEO_DX is missing type 1 if the respondent skipped the gate question */

Set MEO_D1 to **missing1** IF (RD1 = **–5**)

/* MEO_DX occurred if the respondent indicates "yes" to the gate question, and "yes" to any of the three follow-up items that provide evidence of bias (RDXb, RDXc. RDXd). The last follow-up item (RDXe) cannot be used as direct evidence of discrimination and therefore is not included in these instructions. */

Set MEO_D1 to **1** IF (RD1 = **1** AND (RD1b = **1** OR RD1c = **1** OR RD1d = **1**))

/* MEO_DX did not occur if the respondent indicates "no" to the gate question or does not answer "yes" to any of the three direct evidence follow-up items (RDXb–RDXd) */

Set MEO_D1 to **0** IF (RD1 = **2** OR (RD1b = (**2** OR **–5**) AND RD1c = (**2** OR **–5**) AND RD1d = (**2** OR **–5**))

/* MEO_DX is missing type 4 if the respondent answered "yes" to the gate question and skipped either (1) all three direct evidence follow-up items (RDXb–RDXd), or (2) any two of the three direct evidence follow-up items (RDXb–RDXd) AND responded "no" to one */

Set MEO_D1 to **missing4** IF
(RD1 = **1** AND RD1b = **-5** AND RD1c = **-5** AND RD1d = **-5**)
OR
(RD1 = **1** AND RD1b = **2** AND RD1c = **-5** AND RD1d = **-5**)
OR
(RD1 = **1** AND RD1b = **-5** AND RD1c = **2** AND RD1d = **-5**)
OR
(RD1 = **1** AND RD1b = **-5** AND RD1c = **-5** AND RD1d = **2**)

Definitions for Key Topline Variables

Each derived Key Outcome variable is based on the MEO_HX and MEO_DX variables. General rules for deriving key outcomes are as follows:

1. If the respondent was coded "Yes (1)" to any of the corresponding MEO variables, they are classified as experiencing that type of harassment or discrimination.
2. If the respondent is coded as (a) missing (any type) on half of the corresponding MEO variables or fewer, and (b) as "No (0)" to all of the nonmissing MEO variables, they are classified as not experiencing that type of victimization.
3. If the respondent was coded as missing (any type) on more than half of the corresponding MEO variables, they are classified as missing on that measure of victimization.

Definition of Any_MEO_Violation

/* initialize new variable with all missing values */
Set Any_MEO_Violation to **tempmissing**
/* Any_MEO_Violation occurred if any MEO_H1 to MEO_H12 or MEO_D1 to MEO_D12 occurred */
Set Any_MEO_Violation to **1** IF (MEO_H1 = **1** OR MEO_H2 = **1** OR MEO_H3 = **1** OR MEO_H4 = **1** OR MEO_H5 = **1** OR MEO_H6 = **1** OR MEO_H7 = **1** OR MEO_H8 = **1** OR MEO_H9 = **1** OR MEO_H10 = **1** OR MEO_H11 = **1** OR MEO_H12 = **1** OR MEO_D1 = **1** OR MEO_D2 = **1** OR MEO_D3 = **1** OR MEO_D4 = **1** OR MEO_D5 = **1** OR MEO_D6 = **1** OR

MEO_D7 = **1** OR MEO_D8 = **1** OR MEO_D9 = **1** OR MEO_D10 = **1** OR MEO_D11 = **1** OR MEO_D12 = **1**)

/* Any_MEO_Violation did not occur if the respondent (a) is missing on less than half of the MEO variables, and (b) was coded "no" on all nonmissing MEO variables */

Set MEO_MIS to the number of codes across 24 variables (MEO_H1 through MEO_H12 AND MEO_D1 through MEO_D12) = **missing1** OR **missing2** OR **missing3**

Set MEO_NO to the number of codes across 24 variables (MEO_H1 through MEO_H12 AND MEO_D1 through MEO_D12) = **0**

Set Any_MEO_Violation to **0** IF (MEO_MIS ≤ **12** AND (MEO_MIS + MEO_NO = **24**))

/* Any_MEO_Violation is missing if the respondent (a) is missing on more than half of the 24 MEO variables, and (b) was coded "no" on all nonmissing MEO variables */

Set Any_MEO_Violation to **missing** IF (Any_MEO_Violation NE **1** AND MEO_MIS > **12**)

Definition of Any_Harass

/* initialize new variable with all missing values */

Set Any_Harass to **tempmissing**

/* Any_Harass occurred if any of MEO_H1 through MEO_H12 occurred */

Set Any_Harass to **1** IF (MEO_H1 = **1** OR MEO_H2 = **1** OR MEO_H3 = **1** OR MEO_H4 = **1** OR MEO_H5 = **1** OR MEO_H6 = **1** OR MEO_H7 = **1** OR MEO_H8 = **1** OR MEO_H9 = **1** OR MEO_H10 = **1** OR MEO_H11 = **1** OR MEO_H12 = **1**)

/* Any_Harass did not occur if the respondent (a) is missing half of the MEO_H items or fewer, and (b) was coded on "no" on all nonmissing MEO_H variables */

Set Harass_MIS to the number of codes across 12 variables (MEO_H1 through MEO_H12) = **missing1** OR **missing2** OR **missing3**

Set Harass_NO to the number of codes across 12 variables (MEO_H1 through MEO_H12) = **0**

Set Any_Harass to **0** IF (Harass_MIS ≤ **6** AND (Harass_MIS + Harass_NO = **12**))

/* Any_Harass is missing if respondent (a) is missing on more than half of the 12 MEO_H variables, and (b) was coded "no" on all nonmissing MEO_H variables */

Set Any_Harass to **missing** IF (Any_Harass NE **1** AND Harass_MIS > **6**)

Definition of Any_Discrim

/* initialize new variable with all missing values */

Set Any_Discrim to **tempmissing**

/* Any_Discrim occurred if any of MEO_D1 through MEO_D12 occurred */

Set Any_Discrim to **1** IF (MEO_D1 = **1** OR MEO_D2 = **1** OR MEO_D3 = **1** OR MEO_D4 = **1** OR MEO_D5 = **1** OR MEO_D6 = **1** OR MEO_D7 = **1** OR MEO_D8 = **1** OR MEO_D9 = **1** OR MEO_D10 = **1** OR MEO_D11 = **1** OR MEO_D12 = **1**)

/* Any_Discrim did not occur if respondent (a) is missing half of the MEO_D items or fewer, and (b) was coded "no" on all nonmissing MEO_D variables */

Set Discrim_MIS to the number of codes across 12 variables (MEO_D1 through MEO_D12) = **missing1** OR **missing4**

Set Discrim_NO to the number of codes across 12 variables (MEO_D1 through MEO_D12) = **0**

Set Any_Discrim to 0 IF (Discrim_MIS ≤ 6 AND (Discrim_MIS + Discrim_NO = **12**))

/* Any_Discrim is missing if the respondent (a) is missing on more than half of the 11 MEO_D variables, and (b) was coded "no" on all nonmissing MEO_D variables */

Set Any_Discrim to **missing** IF (Any_Discrim NE **1** AND Discrim_MIS > **6**)

Number of Military Equal Opportunity Violations Experienced in the Past Year

Military leaders and decisionmakers will likely be most interested in estimates describing the percentage of service members who experienced racial/ethnic harassment or discrimination (see derived variables discussed earlier). A useful adjunct to these percentage-affected estimates is a count of the number of types of MEO violations each affected service member experienced. A service member who experienced one type of MEO violation may have qualitatively different needs from a service member who experienced five types of MEO violations in the past year.

Number_MEO_Harass: Number of Racial/Ethnic Harassment Violations Experienced

/* Variable creates a sum of racial/ethnic harassment violations (MEO_H1 through MEO_H12) experienced and can range from 0 to 12. The computation relies on a mean across items in order to impute missing values based on the probability with which they are expected to be endorsed */

/* initialize new variable with all missing values */

Set number_MEO_Harass to **tempmissing**

/* Restrict variable to those with nonmissing values for Any_Harass */

Set number_MEO_Harass to **missing** IF Any_Harass NE (**0** or **1**)

/* Computes sum of racial/ethnic harassment violations. Imputes missing values */

Set number_MEO_Harass to (mean(MEO_H1, MEO_H2, MEO_H3, MEO_H4, MEO_H5, MEO_H6, MEO_H7, MEO_H8, MEO_H9, MEO_H10, MEO_H11, MEO_H12) * 12)

Number_MEO_Discrim: Number of Racial/Ethnic Discrimination Violations Experienced

/* Variable creates a sum of racial/ethnic discrimination violations (MEO_D1 through MEO_D12) experienced that can range from 0 to 12. The computation relies on a mean across items in order to impute missing values based on the probability with which they are expected to be endorsed */

/* initialize new variable with all missing values */

Set number_MEO_Discrim to **tempmissing**

/* Restrict variable to those with nonmissing values for Any_Discrim */

Set number_MEO_Discrim to **missing** IF Any_Discrim NE (**0** or **1**)

/* Computes sum of racial/ethnic discrimination violations. Imputes missing values */

Set number_MEO_Discrim to (mean(MEO_D1, MEO_D2, MEO_D3, MEO_D4, MEO_D5, MEO_D6, MEO_D7, MEO_D8, MEO_D9, MEO_D10, MEO_D11, MEO_D12) * 12)

Number_MEO: Number of Military Equal Opportunity Violations Experienced

/* Variable creates a sum of MEO violations experienced that can range from 0 to 23. The computation relies on a mean across items in order to impute missing values based on the probability with which they are expected to be endorsed */

/* initialize new variable with all missing values */

Set number_MEO to **tempmissing**

/* Restrict variable to those with nonmissing values for Any_MEO_Violation */

Set number_MEO to **missing** IF Any_MEO_Violation NE (**0** or **1**)

/* Computes sum of MEO violations. Imputes missing values */

Set number_MEO to (mean(MEO_H1, MEO_H2, MEO_H3, MEO_H4, MEO_H5, MEO_H6, MEO_H7, MEO_H8, MEO_H9, MEO_H10, MEO_H11, MEO_H12, MEO_D1, MEO_D2, MEO_D3, MEO_D4, MEO_D5, MEO_D6, MEO_D7, MEO_D8, MEO_D9, MEO_D10, MEO_D11, MEO_D12) * 23)

Definitions for Inappropriate Workplace Behavior Variables

The topline variables just described can be used to categorize respondents as either experiencing an MEO violation or not. Leaders and decisionmakers may also want to know the percentage of service members who experienced inappropriate workplace behaviors in the past year regardless of whether the experiences rose to the level of an MEO violation. These experiences may still represent a threat to good order and discipline and will be important to track. The derived variables that follow include all people who endorsed experiencing an inappropriate workplace behavior (H1–H12, RD1–RD11) *whether or not* that experience was ultimately categorized as an MEO violation.

Definition of Any_workplaceProblem_Harass

/* initialize new variable with all missing values */

Set Any_workplaceProblem_Harass to **tempmissing**

/* Any_workplaceProblem_Harass occurred if any of H1 through H12 occurred */

Set Any_workplaceProblem_Harass to **1** IF (H1 = **1** OR H2 = **1** OR H3 = **1** OR H4 = **1** OR H5 = **1** OR H6 = **1** OR H7 = **1** OR H8 = **1** OR H9 = **1** OR H10 = **1** OR H11 = **1** OR H12a = **1**)

/* Any_workplaceProblem_Harass did not occur if respondent (a) is missing half of the Harassment items or fewer, and (b) responded "no" to all unskipped items */

Set workplaceProblem_Harass_MIS to the number of codes across 12 variables (H1, H2, H3, H4, H5, H6, H7, H8, H9, H10, H11, (H12 OR H12a)) = **-5**

Set workplaceProblem_Harass_NO to the number of codes across 12 variables (H1, H2, H3, H4, H5, H6, H7, H8, H9, H10, H11, (H12 OR H12a)) = **2**

Set Any_workplaceProblem_Harass to **0** IF (workplaceProblem_Harass_MIS ≤ **6** AND (workplaceProblem_Harass_MIS + workplace Problem_Harass_NO = **12**))

/* Any_workplaceProblem_Harass missing */

Set Any_workplaceProblem_Harass to **missing** IF (Any_workplace Problem_Harass NE **1** AND workplaceProblem_Harass_MIS > **6**)

Definition of Any_workplaceProblem_Discrim

/* initialize new variable with all missing values */

Set Any_workplaceProblem_Discrim to **tempmissing**

/* Any_workplaceProblem_Discrim occurred if any of RD1 through RD12 occurred */

Set Any_workplaceProblem_Discrim to **1** IF (RD1 = **1** OR RD2 = **1** OR RD3 = **1** OR RD4 = **1** OR RD5 = **1** OR RD6 = **1** OR RD7 = **1** OR RD8 = **1** OR RD9 = **1** OR RD10 = **1** OR RD11 = **1** OR RD12 = **1**)

/* Any_workplaceProblem_Discrim did not occur if respondent (a) is missing half of the RD items or fewer, and (b) responded "no" to all unskipped items */

Set workplaceProblem_Discrim_MIS to the number of missing codes across 12 variables (RD1 through RD12) = **–5**

Set workplaceProblem_Discrim_NO to the number of "no" codes across 12 variables (RD1 through RD12) = **2**

Set Any_workplaceProblem_Discrim to **0** IF (workplaceProblem_Discrim_MIS ≤ **6** AND (workplaceProblem_Discrim_MIS + workplace Problem_Disrim_NO = **12**))

/* Any_workplaceProblem_Discrim missing */

Set Any_workplaceProblem_Discrim to **missing** IF (Any_workplace Problem_Discrim NE **1** AND workplaceProblem_Discrim_MIS > **6**)

Abbreviations

DMDC	Defense Manpower Data Center
DoD	U.S. Department of Defense
DoDD	Department of Defense Directive
EEOC	U.S. Equal Employment Opportunity Commission
MEO	Military Equal Opportunity
MOS	military occupational specialty
ODMEO	Office of Diversity Management and Equal Opportunity
OPA	Office of People Analytics
RMWS	RAND Military Workplace Study
WEOA	Workplace and Equal Opportunity Survey of Active Duty Members
WEOR	Workplace and Equal Opportunity Survey of Reserve Component Members
WGR	Workplace and Gender Relations

Bibliography

Alwin, Duane F., "How Good Is Survey Measurement? Assessing the Reliability and Validity of Survey Measures," in Peter V. Marsden and James D. Wright, eds., *Handbook of Survey Research*, Bingely: Emerald Group Publishing, 2010, pp. 405–434.

Austin, L., Message to the Force, March 4, 2021. As of April 20, 2021: https://media.defense.gov/2021/Mar/04/2002593656/-1/-1/0/SECRETARY-LLOYD-J-AUSTIN-III-MESSAGE-TO-THE-FORCE.PDF

Bowen, Shelley, and Anthony B. Zwi, "Pathways to 'Evidence-Informed' Policy and Practice: A Framework for Action," *PLOS Medicine*, Vol. 2, No. 7, 2005, pp. 600–605.

Brondolo, Elizabeth, Kim P. Kelly, Vonetta Coakley, Tamar Gordon, Shola Thompson, Erika Levy, Andrea Cassells, Jonathan N. Tobin, Monica Sweeney, and Richard J. Contrada, "The Perceived Ethnic Discrimination Questionnaire: Development and Preliminary Validation of a Community Version," *Journal of Applied Social Psychology*, Vol. 35, No. 2, February 2005, pp. 335–365.

Brown, Tony N., "Measuring Self-Perceived Racial and Ethnic Discrimination in Social Surveys," *Sociological Spectrum*, Vol. 21, No. 3, 2001, pp. 377–392.

Burlington Industries, Inc. v. Ellerth, 524 U.S. 742 (1998). As of June 6, 2016: https://scholar.google.com/scholar_case?case=2707173104214869053&hl=en&as_sdt=6&as_vis=1&oi=scholarr

Campanelli, Pamela, "Testing Survey Questions," in Edith D. de Leeuw, Joop J. Hox, and Don A. Dillman, eds., *International Handbook of Survey Methodology*, New York: Lawrence Erlbaum Associates, 2008, pp. 176–199.

CNN, "CNN Poll 2006-030: Bush Administration/President Election/Racial Bias," USORCCNN2006-030, telephone interviews with national adult sample of 1,207 people, December 5–7, 2006.

Collado-Proctor, Shirley M., "The Perceived Racism Scale for Latina/os: A Multidimensional Assessment of the Experience of Racism Among Latina/os," thesis, Duke University, December 1998.

Crano, William D., Marilynn B. Brewer, and Andrew Lac, *Principles and Methods of Social Research*, 3rd ed., New York: Routledge, 2015.

Daniel, Samantha, Yvette Claros, Natalie Namrow, Michael Siebel, Amy Campbell, David McGrath, and Ashlea Klahr, *2017 Workplace and Equal Opportunity Survey of Active Duty Members: Executive Report*, Alexandria, Va.: Office of People Analytics, 2019.

Daniel, Samantha, Natalie Namrow, Michael Siebel, and Carol Newell, *2015 Workplace and Equal Opportunity Survey of Reserve Component Members: Overview Report*, Alexandria, Va.: Office of People Analytics, 2018.

Defense Equal Opportunity Management Institute, *Our Mission*, Patrick Air Force Base, Fla., ca. 2013.

Defense Manpower Data Center, *2011 Workplace and Equal Opportunity Survey of Reserve Component Members: Statistical Methodology Report*, Alexandria, Va., Report 2012-054, September 2012a. As of August 23, 2021: https://apps.dtic.mil/sti/pdfs/ADA602627.pdf

———, *2012 Workplace and Gender Relations Survey of Active Duty Members: Statistical Methodology Report*, Alexandria, Va., Report 2012-067, December 2012b.

———, *2011 Workplace and Equal Opportunity Survey of Reserve Component Members: Overview Report*, Note 2013-003, February 26, 2014a. As of July 2, 2017: https://www.opa.mil/research-analysis/quality-of-work-life/workplace-climate/2011-workplace-and-equal-opportunity-survey-of-reserve-component-members/2011-workplace-and-equal-opportunity-survey-of-reserve-component-members-overview-report

———, *2011 Workplace and Equal Opportunity Survey of Reserve Component Members: Tabulations of Responses*, Alexandria, Va., Report 2012-055, March 2014b. As of August 23, 2021: https://dwp.dmdc.osd.mil/dwp/api/download?fileName=WEOR1101_TabVolume.pdf&groupName=pubOpSurResComp

Department of Defense Inspector General, Anti-Harassment Policy Statement, Alexandria, Va., September 20, 2019.

DMDC—*See* Defense Manpower Data Center.

DoD—*See* U.S. Department of Defense.

EEOC—*See* U.S. Equal Employment Opportunity Commission.

Ensher, Ellen A., Elisa J. Grant-Vallone, and Stewart I. Donaldson, "Effects of Perceived Discrimination on Job Satisfaction, Organizational Commitment, Organizational Citizenship Behavior, and Grievances," *Human Resource Development Quarterly*, Vol. 12, No. 1, Spring 2001, pp. 53–72.

Faragher v. City of Boca Raton, 524 U.S. 775 (1998).

Fernandez, Conrad V., Eric Kodish, and Charles Weijer, "Informing Study Participants of Research Results: An Ethical Imperative," *IRB: Ethics and Human Research*, Vol. 25, No. 3, May–June 2003, pp. 12–19.

Fitzgerald, Louise F., Suzanne Swan, and Karla Fischer, "Why Didn't She Just Report Him? The Psychological and Legal Implications of Women's Responses to Sexual Harassment," *Journal of Social Issues*, Vol. 51, No. 1, Spring 1995, pp. 117–138.

Fitzgerald, Louise F., Suzanne Swan, and Vicki Magley, "But Was It Really Sexual Harassment? Legal, Behavioral, and Psychological Definitions of the Workplace Victimization of Women," in William O'Donohue, ed., *Sexual Harassment: Theory, Research, and Treatment*, Needham Heights, Mass.: Allyn and Bacon, 1997, pp. 3–28.

Gagnon, Michelle L., "Moving Knowledge to Action Through Dissemination and Exchange," *Journal of Clinical Epidemiology*, Vol. 64, No. 1, January 2011, pp. 25–31.

Gallup Organization, *Employee Discrimination in the Workplace*, Washington, D.C., December 8, 2005. As of August 2, 2105:
http://media.gallup.com/government/PDF/Gallup_Discrimination_Report_Final.pdf

Gonzalez v. Department of the Army, 718 F.2d 926 (9th Circuit, 1983).

Harrell, S. P., *The Racism and Life Experience Scales (RaLES-Revised)*, Malibu, Calif.: Pepperdine University, unpublished manuscript, 1997.

House, James S., *Americans' Changing Lives: Waves I, II, III, IV, and V, 1986, 1989, 1994, 2002, and 2011 (ICPSR 4690)*, Ann Arbor, Mich.: Inter-University Consortium for Political and Social Research, ICPSR04690-v7, September 9, 2014. As of June 4, 2016:
http://www.icpsr.umich.edu/icpsrweb/NACDA/studies/4690

Huynh, Virginia W., "Ethnic Microaggressions and the Depressive and Somatic Symptoms of Latino and Asian American Adolescents," *Journal of Youth and Adolescence*, Vol. 41, No. 7, July 2012, pp. 831–846.

Ibañez, Gladys E., Barbara Van Oss Marin, Stephen A. Flores, Gregorio Millett, and Rafael M. Diaz, "General and Gay-Related Racism Experienced by Latino Gay Men," *Cultural Diversity and Ethnic Minority Psychology*, Vol. 15, No. 3, July 2009, pp. 215–222.

Jones, James M., *Prejudice and Racism*, 2nd ed., New York: McGraw-Hill Companies, 1997.

Jones, James M., John F. Dovidio, and Deborah L. Vietze, *The Psychology of Diversity: Beyond Prejudice and Racism*, Chichester, England: Wiley Blackwell, 2014.

Karuppan, Corinne M., and Mahua Barari, "Perceived Discrimination and International Students' Learning: An Empirical Investigation," *Journal of Higher Education Policy and Management*, Vol. 33, No. 1, February 2011, pp. 67–83.

Keller, Kirsten M., Miriam Matthews, Kimberly Curry Hall, William Marcellino, Jacqueline A. Mauro, and Nelson Lim, *Hazing in the U.S. Armed Forces: Recommendations for Hazing Prevention Policy and Practice*, Santa Monica, Calif.: RAND Corporation, RR-941-OSD, 2015. As of June 5, 2016:
http://www.rand.org/pubs/research_reports/RR941.html

Krieger, Nancy, Kevin Smith, Deepa Naishadham, Cathy Hartman, and Elizabeth M. Barbeau, "Experiences of Discrimination: Validity and Reliability of a Self-Report Measure for Population Health Research on Racism and Health," *Social Science and Medicine*, Vol. 61, No. 7, October 2005, pp. 1576–1596.

Krosnick, Jon A., "Survey Research," *Annual Review of Psychology*, Vol. 50, February 1999, pp. 537–567.

Krosnick, Jon A., and Stanley Presser, "Question and Questionnaire Design," in Peter V. Marsden and James D. Wright, eds., *Handbook of Survey Research*, 2nd ed., Bingley, England: Emerald, 2010, pp. 263–314.

Lewis, Duncan, and Rod Gunn, "Workplace Bullying in the Public Sector: Understanding the Racial Dimension," *Public Administration*, Vol. 85, No. 3, September 2007, pp. 641–665.

Lomas, Jonathan, *Improving Research Dissemination and Uptake in the Health Sector: Beyond the Sound of One Hand Clapping*, Hamilton, Ont.: McMaster University Centre for Health Economics and Policy Analyses, November 1997.

Loosemore, M., and D. W. Chau, "Racial Discrimination Towards Asian Operatives in the Australian Construction Industry," *Construction Management and Economics*, Vol. 20, No. 1, 2002, pp. 91–102.

MacNeil, S. Danielle, and Conrad V. Fernandez, "Attitudes of Research Ethics Board Chairs Towards Disclosure of Research Results to Participants: Results of a National Survey," *Journal of Medical Ethics*, Vol. 33, No. 9, 2007, pp. 549–553.

Marcus, Ann, Larry C. Mullins, Kimberly P. Brackett, Zongli Tang, Annette M. Allen, and Daniel W. Pruett, "Perceptions of Racism on Campus," *College Student Journal*, Vol. 37, No. 4, December 2003, pp. 611–626.

Miller, Victoria A., William W. Reynolds, Richard F. Ittenbach, Mary Frances Luce, Tom L. Beauchamp, and Robert M. Nelson, "Challenges in Measuring a New Construct: Perception of Voluntariness for Research and Treatment Decision Making," *Journal of Empirical Research on Human Research Ethics*, Vol. 4, No. 3, September 2009, pp. 21–31.

Morral, Andrew R., Kristie L. Gore, and Terry L. Schell, eds., *Sexual Assault and Sexual Harassment in the U.S. Military*, Vol. 1: *Design of the 2014 RAND Military Workplace Study*, Santa Monica, Calif.: RAND Corporation, RR-870/1-OSD, 2014. As of June 5, 2016:
http://www.rand.org/pubs/research_reports/RR870z1.html

Nadal, Kevin L., "The Racial and Ethnic Microaggressions Scale (REMS): Construction, Reliability, and Validity," *Journal of Counseling Psychology*, Vol. 58, No. 4, October 2011, pp. 470–480.

Namrow, Natalie, Elizabeth Van Winkle, Lisa Davis, and Phil Masui, *2013 Workplace and Equal Opportunity Survey of Active Duty Members: Overview Report*, Alexandria, Va.: Defense Manpower Data Center, Report 2014-040, October 1, 2014. As of August 23, 2021:
https://apps.dtic.mil/sti/pdfs/ADA628536.pdf

Nobles, Melissa, *Shades of Citizenship: Race and the Census in Modern Politics*, Stanford, Calif.: Stanford University Press, 2000.

Office of Management and Budget, *Standards and Guidelines for Statistical Surveys*, Washington, D.C., September 2006.

Olson, Kristen, "An Examination of Questionnaire Evaluation by Expert Reviewers," *Field Methods*, Vol. 22, No. 4, 2010, pp. 295–318.

Omi, Michael, and Howard Winant, *Racial Formation in the United States*, London: Routledge, 2014.

Ormerod, Alayne J., Angela K. Lawson, Maria C. Lytell, Caroline Vaile Wright, Christopher Nye, Leigh Ann Perry, Fritz Drasgow, Louise F. Fitzgerald, Catherine Kusznir, and Danielle Rynczak, *2005 Workplace and Equal Opportunity Survey of Active-Duty Members: Report on Scales and Measures*, Arlington, Va.: Defense Manpower Data Center, Report 2007-004, June 2007. As of August 23, 2021:
https://apps.dtic.mil/sti/pdfs/ADA469773.pdf

Pew Research Center, *2007 National Survey of Latinos: As Illegal Immigration Issue Heats Up, Hispanics Feel a Chill*, Washington, D.C., December 13, 2007. As of June 5, 2016:
http://www.pewhispanic.org/2007/12/13/2007-national-survey-of-latinos-as-illegal-immigration-issue-heats-up-hispanics-feel-a-chill/

———, *The Rise of Asian Americans*, updated ed., April 4, 2013. As of June 5, 2016:
http://www.pewsocialtrends.org/2012/06/19/the-rise-of-asian-americans/

Presser, Stanley, and Johnny Blair, "Survey Pretesting: Do Different Methods Produce Different Results?" *Sociological Methodology*, Vol. 24, 1994, pp. 73–104.

Public Law 88-352, Civil Rights Act of 1964, July 2, 1964. As of June 6, 2016:
https://www.gpo.gov/fdsys/granule/STATUTE-78/STATUTE-78-Pg241/content-detail.html

Raver, J. L., and L. H. Nishii, "Ethnic and Gender Harassment Scales [Database Record]," *PsycTESTS*, 2010.

Rhead, Rebecca D., Zoe Chui, Ioannis Bakolis, Billy Gazard, Hannah Harwood, Shirlee MacCrimmon, Charlotte Woodhead, and Stephani L. Hatch, "Impact of Workplace Discrimination and Harassment Among National Health Service Staff Working in London Trusts: Results from the TIDES Study," *BJPsych Open* 7, no. 1, 2021.

Roberson, Loriann, Carol T. Kulik, and Molly B. Pepper, "Using Needs Assessment to Resolve Controversies in Diversity Training Design," *Group and Organization Management*, Vol. 28, No. 1, March 2003, pp. 148–174.

Roper v. Department of Army, 832 F.2d 247 (2nd Cir., 1987).

Rothgeb, Jennifer, Gordon Willis, and Barbara Forsyth, *Questionnaire Pretesting Method: Do Different Techniques and Different Organizations Produce Similar Results?* Washington, D.C.: U.S. Census Bureau, Statistical Research Division, March 21, 2005. As of August 3, 2015: https://www.census.gov/srd/papers/pdf/rsm2005-02.pdf

Sanchez, Juan I., and Petra Brock, "Outcomes of Perceived Discrimination Among Hispanic Employees: Is Diversity Management a Luxury or a Necessity?" *Academy of Management Journal*, Vol. 39, No. 3, June 1996, pp. 704–719.

Savage, Jeanne E., and Briana Mezuk, "Psychosocial and Contextual Determinants of Alcohol and Drug Use Disorders in the National Latino and Asian American Study," *Drug and Alcohol Dependence*, Vol. 139, June 1, 2014, pp. 71–78.

Settles, Isis H., NiCole T. Buchanan, and Stevie C. Y. Yap, "Race/Color Discrimination," in Michele Antoinette Paludi, Carmen A. Paludi, and Eros DeSouza, eds., *Praeger Handbook on Understanding and Preventing Workplace Discrimination*, Vol. 1: *Legal, Management, and Social Science Perspectives*, Santa Barbara, Calif.: Praeger, 2011, pp. 133–156.

Shields, Michael A., and Stephen Wheatley Price, "Racial Harassment, Job Satisfaction and Intentions to Quit: Evidence from the British Nursing Profession," *Economica*, Vol. 69, No. 274, May 2002, pp. 295–326.

Sidanius, Jim, and Felicia Pratto, *Social Dominance: An Intergroup Theory of Social Hierarchy and Oppression*, New York: Cambridge University Press, 1999.

Stewart, Phil, "Exclusive: Long-Withheld Pentagon Survey Shows Widespread Racial Discrimination, Harassment," Reuters, January 14, 2021.

Triana, María del Carmen, Mevan Jayasinghe, and Jenna R. Pieper, "Perceived Workplace Racial Discrimination and Its Correlates: A Meta-Analysis," *Journal of Organizational Behavior*, Vol. 36, No. 4, May 2015, pp. 491–513.

Under Secretary of Defense for Personnel and Readiness, *Department of Defense Military Equal Opportunity (MEO) Program*, Washington, D.C., Department of Defense Directive 1350.2, August 18, 1995, incorporating change 2, June 8, 2015.

———, Diversity Management and Equal Opportunity in the DoD, Washington, D.C., Department of Defense Directive 1020.02E, June 8, 2015, incorporating change 2, June 1, 2018.

———, *Harassment Prevention and Response for DoD Civilian Employees*, Washington, D.C., Department of Defense Instruction 1020.03, June 30, 2020a.

———, *Department of Defense Military Equal Opportunity Program*, Washington, D.C., Department of Defense Instruction 1350.02, September 4, 2020b.

———, *Harassment Prevention and Response in the Armed Forces*, Washington, D.C., Department of Defense Instruction 1020.03, February 8, 2018, incorporating change 1, December 29, 2020c.

U.S. Code, Title 10, Armed Forces, Subtitle A, General Military Law, Part I, Organization and General Military Powers, Chapter 23, Miscellaneous Studies and Reports, Section 481, Racial and Ethnic Issues; Gender Issues: Surveys. As of June 6, 2016:
https://www.gpo.gov/fdsys/granule/USCODE-2010-title10/USCODE-2010-title10-subtitleA-partI-chap23-sec481

U.S. Department of Defense, *Manual for Courts-Martial United States*, 2012 ed., Washington, D.C., April 5, 2012a. As of October 3, 2014:
http://www.loc.gov/rr/frd/Military_Law/pdf/MCM-2012.pdf

———, *Diversity and Inclusion Strategic Plan: 2012–2017*, Washington, D.C., April 19, 2012b. As of June 5, 2016:
http://diversity.defense.gov/Portals/51/Documents/DoD_Diversity_Strategic_Plan_%20final_as%20of%2019%20Apr%2012[1].pdf

U.S. Equal Employment Opportunity Commission, "Charge Statistics FY 1997 Through FY 2020," undated a. As of April 20, 2021:
http://www.eeoc.gov/eeoc/statistics/enforcement/charges.cfm

———, "Harassment," undated b. As of August 5, 2015:
http://www.eeoc.gov/laws/types/harassment.cfm

———, "New Gallup Poll on Employment Discrimination Shows Progress, Problems 40 Years After Founding of EEOC," press release, December 8, 2005. As of August 2, 2015:
http://www.eeoc.gov/eeoc/newsroom/release/12-8-05.cfm

Wei, Meifen, Kenneth T. Wang, and Tsun-Yao Ku, "A Development and Validation of the Perceived Language Discrimination Scale," *Cultural Diversity and Ethnic Minority Psychology*, Vol. 18, No. 4, October 2012, pp. 340–351.

Williams, David R., Yan Yu, James S. Jackson, and Norman B. Anderson, "Racial Differences in Physical and Mental Health: Socio-Economic Status, Stress and Discrimination," *Journal of Health Psychology*, Vol. 2, No. 3, July 1997, pp. 335–351.

Willis, Gordon B., Susan Schechter, and Karen Whitaker, "A Comparison of Cognitive Interviewing, Expert Review, and Behavior Coding: What Do They Tell Us?" paper presented at Joint Statistical Meetings, Baltimore, Md., Proceedings of Survey Research Methods Section of the American Statistical Association, Washington, D.C.: American Statistical Association, 1999, pp. 28–37.

Wilson, Paul M., Mark Petticrew, Michael W. Calnan, and Irwin Nazareth, "Does Dissemination Extend Beyond Publication: A Survey of a Cross Section of Public Funded Research in the UK," *Implementation Science*, Vol. 5, 2010.